COMPLETE
DESSERT COOKBOOK

**75 Years of Good Eating from the
Famous C_{and}H Sugar Kitchen**

A Benjamin Company/Rutledge Book

QE This symbol which appears throughout the book, indicates that a recipe is quick and easy to prepare.

COMPLETE DESSERT COOKBOOK was prepared under the direction of Nancy F. Newland of C and H Sugar Co., based on recipes from the C and H Sugar Kitchen.

Photography: All color photography by Gordon E. Smith
except: Cover and page 212: Skelton Photography
Page 31: Walter Swarthout Studios
Page 181: Rudolph Legname

Prepared and produced by Rutledge Books, Inc.
Published by The Benjamin Company, Inc.
485 Madison Avenue, New York, N.Y. 10022

Library of Congress Catalog Card Number 80-69641
International Standard Book Number: 0-87502-087-9

Printed in the United States of America
First Printing: February, 1981

CONTENTS

WHAT'S YOUR SUGAR I.Q.?

Q. What is sugar?

A. A pure carbohydrate, sugar is one of the cheapest sources of food energy. Carbohydrates in the form of sugar and starches provide almost half the energy the human body needs to live and work. In a healthy well-balanced diet, sugar allows protein to perform its vital body-building functions more efficiently.

Q. Is it just a sweetener?

A. Sugar's properties have made it one of the world's most versatile ingredients in food preparation. It is essential to the baking, fermentation and preservation processes.

Sugar is a necessary ingredient in cookies, where it creates just the right crust, flavor and texture; in breads, where it softens the gluten in flour and feeds yeast so the dough will rise; in custards, where it tenderizes the protein in egg; and in the canning of fruits and vegetables, where sugar acts as a natural preservative and inhibitor of bacteria.

Q. Is sugar fattening?

A. Gram for gram, sugar contributes the same number of calories—units of energy—as protein and half that of fat. A teaspoon of refined white cane sugar contains only 16 calories.

Q. Is honey "healthier" than sugar?

A. Honey is essentially an invert sugar and the human body reacts similarly to all forms of sugar. Honey has less calcium, phosphorus and iron than brown sugar, but it has more calories than equal amounts of granulated, powdered or brown sugar.

Q. How is sugar made?

A. All green plants make sugar in their leaves through the process of photosynthesis. Sugarcane, a giant grass which stores sugar in its stalk, thrives in a warm, moist climate such as Hawaii, the nation's largest sugar producing state.

Q. How is sugarcane processed?

A. During its growth cycle, which in Hawaii averages two years, the cane shoots up as high as 20 or 30 feet. At harvest time, the fields are "burned off"—set afire to burn away dry leaves. The tough, waxy sugarcane stalks are then cut and hauled to the mill where heavy iron rollers extract the sugarcane juice. The juice is clarified, concentrated into a thick syrup, then crystallized in a centrifuge.

The remaining crystals, known as raw sugar, are shipped in specially designed ships to the C and H refinery (the world's largest) in Crockett, California. There, white sugar is produced after the raw crystals have been rinsed, dissolved, filtered, recrystallized, washed, centrifuged again and finally dried. Brown sugar is made by restoring a controlled amount of molasses to refined white sugar for flavor and color.

Q. What are the forms of sugar?

A. C and H produces several forms of pure cane sugar for home use:

GRANULATED—the kitchen "workhorse"; contains no additives, keeps indefinitely.

SUPERFINE—tiny crystals dissolve quickly; excellent for iced drinks, meringues and high, airy sponge cakes.

POWDERED—sometimes called "confectioner's" sugar; contains a small amount of cornstarch to prevent caking; used for icings, frostings and uncooked candies.

GOLDEN BROWN—a "soft" sugar used in baking and making glazes, condiments and butterscotch.

DARK BROWN—rich molasses taste; used for full-flavored foods such as baked beans and gingerbread.

CUBES/CUBELETS—compressed white sugar in two cube sizes to be served with hot beverages.

Q. How can hardened brown sugar be softened?

A. Brown sugar should be stored in tightly closed, rustproof containers to retain the sugar's natural moisture. If the sugar should dry out and harden, place a dampened (not wet) wad of paper towel on a piece of plastic wrap or foil on top of the sugar. Cover the container tightly and store at least 8 hours.

If you're ready to cook and can't wait 8 hours, try this fast—but temporary—method: place hardened sugar in a pan in a 300°F oven for about 5 minutes. Use softened sugar quickly, since it hardens again as it cools.

Q. How should powdered sugar be stored?

A. Like its brown cousins, powdered sugar should be stored in airtight containers, but for the opposite reason—to keep moisture out! If powdered sugar does become lumpy, shake the container gently or sift before using. (C and H Pure Cane Powdered Sugar does not normally require sifting.)

Q. Can brown sugar be substituted for granulated in recipes?

A. Yes, if the flavor suits your taste, many quick breads, cookies and cakes may be made with brown sugar. (We don't recommend switching sugars in fine-textured cakes and fancy desserts, though.) Use equal substitutions, but always remember to pack brown sugars firmly when measuring.

Any more questions?

If you have questions about sugar we haven't answered here, write to Jean Porter, Home Economist, C and H Sugar Kitchen, San Francisco, California 94106.

Thank goodness for sugar—thank sugar for goodness!

1 COFFEE BREAKERS

Marvelous breakfasts, breads and snacks

Breakfast, that most important meal of the day, needs an imaginative touch to nudge sleepy heads awake and inspire them to stoke up for an active day. Try offering a variety of interesting fruit and nut breads. They're not only tasty, but highly nutritious. Bake them two or more at a time on a shelf centered in the oven (allow room for heat to circulate on all sides). Freeze extra loaves to use later for brunches, coffee "klatches," bridge parties and snacks.

Pancakes, waffles and muffins bake quickly and can be weekday offerings for breakfast or lunch without fuss if you make your own premix and keep it on the shelf for handy use. Combine the dry ingredients for several batches in a large jar, stir well and cover tightly. Pancake batter can be made the night before and refrigerated (bring it to room temperature before using).

Remember to stir waffle batter and muffin dough only until the flour is dampened—the mixture will be lumpy. Muffin cups do not need greasing if you use paper liners. A good muffin has an evenly rounded top and a coarse but even grain. Overmixing results in an uneven top and grain, with air tunnels pushing through the muffin. Muffins baked in too slow an oven do not peak; baked in too hot an oven, the peak will be off center.

Speaking of oven temperatures, did you know that many newer baking pans require lower heats? If you use glass pans or those with enamel or non-stick coatings, reduce temperature by 25°F or more.

Unfortunately, an inexplicable mystique about yeast breads discourages many a budding chef from experimenting with them.

Shake off all those preconceived ideas about their difficulty. Almost the only thing you can do to ruin a yeast bread is to dissolve the yeast in water that's too hot or to fail to wait until the dough has risen properly. Water should be about 105°F to 110°F and will feel lukewarm if dabbed on the inside of your wrist. The easiest test for properly risen dough is to stick a finger into it. If the impression of your finger remains, the dough is ready for the next step.

Bake yeast breads positioned in the oven so that the top of the loaf pan is at the center of the oven. Bread is done if it sounds hollow when thumped on the bottom crust. Yeast breads keep well and freeze well. Add them to your repertory and see your culinary reputation increase by leaps and bounds.

Hawaiian Fruitcake (page 10)

HAWAIIAN FRUITCAKE

Photograph on page 9

Makes 1 loaf

¾ cup C & H Granulated Sugar

¾ cup all-purpose flour

¾ teaspoon salt

¼ teaspoon EACH baking powder *and* baking soda

2 cups (10 ounces) pitted whole dates

1 cup (8 ounces) glacéed pineapple pieces

1 cup (5 ounces) macadamia nuts (or 2 cups blanched almonds), chopped

3 eggs

½ teaspoon brandy extract

Preheat oven to 300°F. Grease 9x5x3-inch loaf pan and line bottom with greased paper. In large bowl, mix sugar, flour, salt, baking powder and soda. Stir in dates, pineapple and nuts, coating with sugar mixture. Beat eggs until thick and lemon-colored. Fold eggs and brandy extract into fruit mixture. Turn into loaf pan. Bake 1½ hours. Cool in pan 10 minutes, then turn out onto rack and peel off paper to finish cooling. Garnish, if desired, with fruit and nuts. To serve, slice thinly. Keeps well, tightly wrapped, up to 2 months.

Note: C & H Golden Brown Sugar, packed, may be substituted for the granulated.

BANANA BROWN BREAD

Banana contributes moistness, as well as flavor

Makes 1 loaf

¾ cup C & H Brown Sugar, packed
¼ cup shortening
2 eggs
1 cup mashed ripe bananas (2 to 3 medium)
¾ cup whole wheat or graham flour

½ cup chopped walnuts or pecans
1 cup all-purpose flour
2 teaspoons baking powder
½ teaspoon salt
¼ teaspoon baking soda

Preheat oven to 350°F. Grease 9x5x3-inch loaf pan. Mix sugar, shortening and eggs in bowl. Stir in banana, whole wheat flour and nuts. Combine all-purpose flour with baking powder, salt and soda. Add to banana mixture; mix just until dry ingredients are moistened. Pour into loaf pan. Bake 1 hour or until cake tester inserted in center comes out clean. Turn out onto rack to cool.

MANGO BREAD

Exotic tropical flavor in an easy quick bread

Makes 1 loaf

1 cup C & H Granulated Sugar
½ cup (1 stick) butter or margarine, softened
2 eggs
2¼ cups all-purpose flour

1 tablespoon baking powder
½ teaspoon salt
1 cup pureed mangoes (2 to 3 medium)
1 tablespoon lemon juice

Preheat oven to 350°F. Grease and flour 9x5x3-inch loaf pan. Cream sugar and butter until fluffy. Add eggs, 1 at a time, beating well after each addition. Combine flour, baking powder and salt. Blend half the dry ingredients into creamed mixture. Combine mangoes and lemon juice, then stir into batter. Add remaining flour and mix well. Pour into loaf pan. Bake 55 to 60 minutes. Remove from pan and cool on rack.

BROWN SUGAR NUT BREAD

Photograph on page 17

Makes 1 loaf

1 cup C & H Brown
Sugar, packed
2 cups all-purpose flour
1 teaspoon salt
1/2 teaspoon baking soda

1 cup coarsely chopped
walnuts
1 egg, lightly beaten
1 cup buttermilk or sour
milk

Preheat oven to 350°F. Grease 8½x4½x2½-inch loaf pan. Mix sugar, flour, salt, soda and walnuts in bowl. Combine egg and milk. Stir into dry ingredients, mixing just until moistened. Pour into loaf pan. Rest 20 minutes in warm place, then bake 60 to 70 minutes or until cake tester inserted in center comes out clean. Turn out onto rack to cool. Slices easily even while warm.

SPICY APPLE BREAD

Makes 1 loaf

3/4 cup C & H Dark Brown
Sugar, packed
1/2 cup shortening
2 eggs
1 cup coarsely grated raw
apples (about 2
medium)
2 cups all-purpose flour

1 teaspoon EACH baking
powder, salt *and*
cinnamon
1/2 teaspoon EACH baking
soda *and* nutmeg
1/4 teaspoon ground cloves
1/4 cup buttermilk or sour
milk
1/2 cup chopped walnuts

Preheat oven to 350°F. Grease 9x5x3-inch loaf pan. In large bowl, beat sugar, shortening and eggs. Stir in apples. Combine flour, baking powder, salt, cinnamon, soda, nutmeg and cloves. Stir half the flour mixture into apple mixture. Add buttermilk and remaining flour mixture. Stir just until ingredients are moistened. Stir in walnuts. Pour into loaf pan. Bake 55 to 60 minutes or until cake tester inserted in center comes out clean. Turn out onto rack to cool. For easier slicing, cool several hours or overnight.

PUMPKIN BREAD   QE

Moist and spicy, plump with raisins and nuts, this is autumn itself

Makes 1 loaf

1 cup C & H Golden
   Brown Sugar, packed
½ cup C & H Granulated
   Sugar
1 cup cooked or canned
   pumpkin puree
½ cup vegetable oil
2 eggs
2 cups all-purpose flour

1 teaspoon baking soda
½ teaspoon EACH salt,
   nutmeg *and*
   cinnamon
¼ teaspoon ground ginger
1 cup raisins
½ cup chopped nuts
¼ cup water

Preheat oven to 350°F. Grease 9x5x3-inch loaf pan. Mix brown sugar, granulated sugar, pumpkin, oil and eggs until well blended. Combine flour, soda, salt, nutmeg, cinnamon and ginger; stir into pumpkin mixture. Add raisins, nuts and water. Pour into loaf pan. Bake 65 to 75 minutes or until cake tester inserted in center comes out clean. Turn out onto rack to cool thoroughly.

PINEAPPLE COCONUT BREAD   QE

Flavor and aroma of Hawaii, captured in a breakfast loaf

Makes 1 loaf

¾ cup C & H Granulated
   Sugar
¼ cup (½ stick) butter or
   margarine, softened
2 eggs
1 cup (8¾-ounce can)
   crushed pineapple,
   undrained

½ cup grated coconut
2 cups all-purpose flour
1 tablespoon baking
   powder
½ teaspoon salt

Preheat oven to 350°F. Grease 9x5x3-inch loaf pan. In bowl, beat sugar, butter and eggs until smooth and creamy. Stir in pineapple and coconut. Combine flour, baking powder and salt; stir into creamed mixture. Pour into loaf pan. Bake 1 hour. Turn out onto rack to cool.

13

SPICED ZUCCHINI BREAD

The orphan of the garden becomes the star of the breakfast table

Makes 1 loaf

1 cup C & H Granulated Sugar

½ cup (1 stick) butter or margarine, softened

2 eggs

1¾ cups all-purpose flour

½ teaspoon EACH salt, baking soda *and* nutmeg

1 cup finely grated unpeeled zucchini

½ cup chopped walnuts

1 teaspoon vanilla

Preheat oven to 350°F. Grease 9x5x3-inch loaf pan. Cream sugar and butter. Beat in eggs. Combine flour, salt, baking soda and nutmeg. Stir half the dry ingredients into the creamed mixture. Stir in zucchini (batter may look curdled). Stir in remaining dry ingredients, then walnuts and vanilla. Bake 50 to 60 minutes. Turn out onto rack to cool.

DATE-APRICOT-NUT BREAD

Nuts and dried fruit make an appealing wintertime snack

Makes 1 loaf

½ cup dried apricots

1 cup C & H Brown Sugar, packed

½ cup snipped dates

¾ cup coarsely chopped walnuts

3 cups all-purpose flour

1 tablespoon baking powder

1½ teaspoons salt

¼ teaspoon baking soda

1 egg

1½ cups milk

Preheat oven to 350°F. Grease 9x5x3-inch loaf pan. In small bowl, cover apricots with boiling water; let stand 15 minutes. Drain and, with scissors, snip into strips. Combine with sugar, dates, walnuts, flour, baking powder, salt, and soda. Mix egg and milk. Stir into fruit mixture. Pour into loaf pan (batter will be thin). Let stand 20 minutes, then bake 1¼ hours or until cake tester inserted in center comes out clean. Turn out onto rack to cool.

BISHOP'S DATE BREAD

Exceptionally good date nut bread, with a special lemon-chocolate flavor secret

Makes 1 loaf

3/4 cup C & H Golden
  Brown Sugar, packed
1/4 teaspoon salt
6 eggs, separated
1 cup chopped walnuts
1 cup snipped dates
1/2 cup diced candied citron
1 teaspoon grated lemon
  rind
2 ounces unsweetened
  chocolate, grated
1 cup all-purpose flour
  Pinch EACH salt *and*
  cream of tartar

Preheat oven to 300°F. Grease 9x5x3-inch loaf pan and line bottom with greased paper. Gradually beat sugar and salt into egg yolks; continue beating until thick, smooth and lemon-colored. Stir in walnuts, dates, citron, lemon rind and chocolate. Blend in flour. Beat egg whites with salt and cream of tartar until stiff, then fold into flour mixture (yes it will—just keep folding). Pour into loaf pan. Bake 1 1/2 hours. Remove from pan, peel off paper and cool on rack.

BREAKFAST CHEDDAR BREAD

Leftovers—if there are any—make crunchy, delectable toast

Makes 1 loaf

1/2 cup C & H Granulated
  Sugar
1/2 cup shortening
3 eggs
2 cups all-purpose flour
1 tablespoon baking
  powder
3/4 teaspoon salt
1 cup milk
1 cup shredded sharp
  cheddar cheese
1/2 cup chopped nuts

Preheat oven to 375°F. Grease 9x5x3-inch loaf pan. Cream sugar and shortening until fluffy. Add eggs, 1 at a time, beating well after each addition. Combine flour, baking powder and salt. Add alternately to creamed mixture with milk, beginning and ending with dry ingredients. Stir in cheese and nuts. Pour into loaf pan. Bake 1 hour or until cake tester inserted in center comes out clean. Turn out onto rack to cool.

15

SESAME QUICK BREAD

Makes 1 loaf

¾ cup C & H Golden
   Brown Sugar, packed
2 cups whole wheat flour
½ cup unprocessed bran
1 tablespoon baking
   powder
1 teaspoon cinnamon
½ teaspoon salt

1½ cups buttermilk or
   whole milk
¼ cup vegetable oil
1 egg, lightly beaten
3 tablespoons sesame
   seeds, toasted*
Cream Cheese Spread
   (recipe follows)

Preheat oven to 350°F. Grease and flour 8½x4½x2½-inch loaf pan. In large bowl, combine all ingredients except 1 tablespoon sesame seeds and the spread. Stir just until blended. Turn into loaf pan. Sprinkle remaining sesame seeds over top. Bake 1 hour or until cake tester inserted in center comes out clean. Cool 10 minutes in pan. Turn out onto rack to finish cooling. Serve with Cream Cheese Spread.

*Note: To toast sesame seeds, spread in shallow pan and bake, stirring frequently, 8 to 10 minutes in 350°F oven until brown.

Cream Cheese Spread

2 tablespoons C & H
   Golden Brown Sugar
1 package (3 ounces)
   cream cheese,
   softened

1 tablespoon grated
   orange rind
1 tablespoon orange juice

Mix all ingredients until well blended. Refrigerate until ready to serve.

Clockwise from top: Sour Cream Date Muffins (page 23), Granola Bran Muffins (page 22), Brown Sugar Nut Bread (page 12), Cream Cheese Spread and Sesame Quick Bread

COMPLETE DESSERT COOKBOOK

GRANOLA CARROT BREAD

Golden, easy-do loaf the whole family will love

Makes 1 loaf

½ cup C & H Golden
   Brown Sugar, packed
1½ cups granola
1½ cups whole wheat flour
1½ cups grated carrots
½ cup vegetable oil

1 tablespoon baking
   powder
1 teaspoon vanilla
½ teaspoon salt
2 eggs
½ cup milk, buttermilk or
   sour milk

Preheat oven to 350°F. Grease and flour 8½x4½x2½-inch loaf pan. Combine all ingredients in bowl; stir until just mixed. Turn into loaf pan. Bake 55 to 60 minutes or until cake tester inserted in center comes out clean. Cool 10 minutes in pan. Turn out onto rack to finish cooling.

GOLDEN BROWN
BUTTERMILK COFFEE CAKE

A buttery pecan crumb filling provides the special flavor

Makes 12 to 16 servings

¾ cup C & H Golden
   Brown Sugar, packed
½ cup (1 stick) butter,
   softened
3 eggs
3 cups all-purpose flour
2 teaspoons baking
   powder

1 teaspoon baking soda
½ teaspoon salt
1 cup buttermilk
1 teaspoon vanilla
   Pecan Crumb Filling
   (recipe follows)

Preheat oven to 350°F. Grease 3-quart fluted tube pan. Cream sugar, butter and eggs. Combine flour, baking powder, soda and salt. Add alternately with buttermilk to sugar mixture. Stir in vanilla (batter will be thick). Spoon half the batter into pan, then sprinkle with half the Crumb Filling. Repeat. Bake 1 hour. Cool 5 minutes, then invert on rack. Serve warm or cool.

Pecan Crumb Filling

1 cup C & H Golden
    Brown Sugar, packed
¼ cup all-purpose flour

¼ cup (½ stick) butter
⅓ cup minced pecans

Blend sugar and flour. Cut in butter with pastry blender or fingertips until mixture is crumbly. Stir in pecans.

RAISIN YOGURT COFFEE CAKE

Makes 8 to 10 servings

1 cup C & H Golden
    Brown Sugar, packed
½ cup (1 stick) butter or
    margarine, softened
1 teaspoon vanilla
2 eggs
½ cup chopped golden
    raisins

2 cups all-purpose flour
1 teaspoon baking powder
½ teaspoon salt
½ cup plain yogurt
    Walnut Crumb Filling
    (recipe follows)

Preheat oven to 350°F. Grease a 9-inch square pan. Cream sugar, butter and vanilla. Add eggs, 1 at a time, beating well after each addition. Stir in raisins. Combine flour, baking powder and salt. Add to creamed mixture alternately with yogurt, beginning and ending with dry ingredients. Spread half the batter in pan. Sprinkle with half the Crumb Filling. Repeat. Bake 40 minutes. Serve warm or cool.

Note: C & H Granulated Sugar may be substituted for C & H Brown Sugar, milk may be used instead of yogurt, and dates may replace raisins.

Walnut Crumb Filling

½ cup C & H Golden
    Brown Sugar, packed
¼ cup (½ stick) butter or
    margarine

2 teaspoons cinnamon
¾ cup coarsely chopped
    walnuts

Blend all ingredients with pastry blender or fingertips until crumbly.

DELICIOUS PEACH COFFEE CAKE

For an exquisite Sunday brunch, serve with Canadian bacon and shirred eggs

Makes 9 to 12 servings

½ cup C & H Granulated Sugar
1 egg
⅓ cup butter or margarine, melted
¾ cup milk
2 cups all-purpose flour

1 tablespoon baking powder
½ teaspoon salt
Topping (recipe follows)
2 fresh peaches, peeled and sliced, or 1 can (16 ounces) sliced peaches, drained

Preheat oven to 400°F. Grease and flour 9-inch square pan. Beat sugar and egg in large bowl until well mixed. Stir in butter and milk. Combine flour, baking powder and salt; stir into sugar mixture. Spread batter in pan. Sprinkle ¾ of topping mixture on batter; arrange peach slices over top and sprinkle with remaining topping. Bake 30 minutes.

Topping

½ cup C & H Golden Brown Sugar, packed
¼ cup all-purpose flour

1 teaspoon cinnamon
2 tablespoons butter or margarine, softened

Combine sugar, flour and cinnamon. Cut butter into sugar mixture until crumbly.

Delicious Peach Coffee Cake

ON-THE-GO GRANOLA

Once you've tried this, you'll know that homemade is the only way to go

Makes 6½ cups

1 cup C & H Golden
   Brown Sugar, packed
3 cups old-fashioned oats
½ cup wheat germ
½ cup unprocessed bran
½ cup sunflower seeds or
   chopped nuts
   (optional)
¼ cup vegetable oil

⅓ cup mashed banana or 6
   tablespoons (3
   ounces) frozen apple
   or pineapple juice
   concentrate, thawed
1½ teaspoons cinnamon
1 cup seedless dark
   raisins (optional)

Preheat oven to 325°F. In large bowl, lightly mix all ingredients except raisins. Spread on large baking sheet to ½-inch thickness, dividing mixture between 2 baking sheets, if necessary. Bake 30 minutes, stirring every 10 minutes or until chunks *begin* to crisp (they will crisp further while cooling). Stir in raisins. Cool, then store in airtight container in refrigerator.

GRANOLA BRAN MUFFINS

Photograph on page 17

Makes 1 dozen

¼ cup C & H Golden
   Brown Sugar, packed
1 cup granola
¾ cup unprocessed bran
¾ cup whole wheat flour

1 teaspoon EACH baking
   soda *and* cinnamon
½ teaspoon salt
1 egg
¾ cup buttermilk
¼ cup vegetable oil

Preheat oven to 400°F. Grease 12 muffin cups. Combine all ingredients in bowl. Mix just until dry ingredients are moistened. Spoon into muffin cups. Bake 15 minutes or until pick inserted in center comes out clean.

PINEAPPLE BRAN MUFFINS QE

Serve with slices of mild cheese and tall glasses of milk for a delicious, unusual breakfast

Makes 1 dozen

1 cup shredded all-bran cereal
$\frac{1}{2}$ cup milk
1 cup (8$\frac{3}{4}$-ounce can) crushed pineapple, undrained
$\frac{1}{4}$ cup raisins
$\frac{1}{4}$ cup shortening

1 egg
$\frac{1}{2}$ cup C & H Dark Brown Sugar, packed
1 cup all-purpose flour
2 teaspoons baking powder
$\frac{1}{2}$ teaspoon salt
$\frac{1}{4}$ teaspoon baking soda

Preheat oven to 400°F. Combine cereal, milk, pineapple and raisins. Stir in shortening and egg; mix thoroughly. Combine remaining ingredients and add to cereal mixture. Mix until ingredients are moistened. Spoon batter evenly into 12 paper-lined muffin cups. Bake 25 to 30 minutes.

SOUR CREAM DATE MUFFINS

Photograph on page 17

Makes 1 dozen

$\frac{3}{4}$ cup C & H Granulated Sugar
1$\frac{3}{4}$ cups all-purpose flour
1 tablespoon baking powder
$\frac{1}{2}$ teaspoon salt

$\frac{1}{2}$ cup snipped dates
$\frac{1}{2}$ pint (1 cup) sour cream
1 egg
$\frac{1}{2}$ cup (1 stick) butter, melted, cooled
$\frac{1}{2}$ teaspoon cinnamon

Preheat oven to 400°F. Grease 12 muffin cups. Combine $\frac{1}{4}$ cup sugar, the flour, baking powder and salt in bowl. Stir in dates. Combine sour cream, egg and 2 tablespoons of the butter. Stir into dry ingredients, mixing just until moistened. Spoon into muffin cups. Bake 20 minutes or until pick inserted in center comes out clean. Combine $\frac{1}{2}$ cup sugar and the cinnamon in bowl. Dip tops of hot muffins in remaining melted butter, then cinnamon-sugar. Serve warm.

23

CARAMEL NUT WAFFLES

Waffles served with a sauce that would be equally good on pancakes, French toast or ice cream

Makes 6 waffles

3 tablespoons C & H Brown Sugar
2 cups all-purpose flour
1 tablespoon baking powder
3 eggs, separated
1½ cups milk
⅓ cup butter or margarine, melted, cooled

¾ cup coarsely chopped pecans
½ teaspoon salt
⅛ teaspoon cream of tartar
Hot Caramel Sauce (recipe follows)

Preheat waffle iron. Combine sugar, flour and baking powder in bowl. Mix egg yolks, milk and butter. Stir into dry ingredients, mixing just until moistened. Stir in pecans. Beat egg whites with salt and cream of tartar until stiff, then fold into flour mixture. Bake in waffle iron following manufacturer's instructions. Serve with Hot Caramel Sauce.

Hot Caramel Sauce

1¼ cups C & H Granulated Sugar
½ cup water

1 cup heavy cream, heated
½ teaspoon vanilla

Combine sugar and water in heavy skillet and cook, stirring occasionally, over low heat until sugar melts. Raise heat and cook until sugar caramelizes and turns a deep mahogany brown. Stand back (in case mixture splatters) and slowly pour in cream. Stir over low heat until smooth, then mix in vanilla. Keep warm in double boiler. Makes about 2 cups.

Caramel Nut Waffles with Hot Caramel Sauce

SWEDISH PANCAKES

Makes 4 servings

2 tablespoons C & H
  Granulated Sugar
½ teaspoon salt
1⅓ cups all-purpose flour
4 eggs
1 cup milk

2 tablespoons butter,
  melted (optional)
C & H Powdered Sugar
Sweetened fruit or
  preserves

Combine sugar, salt, flour, eggs, milk and butter in blender or food processor. Process until smooth. Rest at room temperature 2 hours. Preheat oven to 200°F. Preheat Swedish section pan, griddle or cast iron skillet. Grease lightly, if necessary. Drop batter by tablespoonfuls into pan. Cook about 3 minutes until bottom browns, then flip pancakes over and brown other side. Keep warm in oven while cooking subsequent batches. Sprinkle with powdered sugar and top with fruit or preserves.

PRUNE KUCHEN

An easy version of a favorite old-world treat

Makes 8 servings

2 tablespoons C & H
  Granulated Sugar
1 cup all-purpose flour
¼ teaspoon salt
½ cup (1 stick) butter or
  margarine, softened

2 cups pitted prunes
  (about 40)
½ cup C & H Granulated
  Sugar
¼ teaspoon cinnamon
2 egg yolks
½ pint (1 cup) sour cream

Preheat oven to 350°F. Grease 8-inch square pan. Combine 2 tablespoons sugar, the flour, salt and butter. Mix with pastry blender or fingertips until mixture resembles coarse meal. Place in pan; pat evenly over bottom and up sides. Place prunes on pastry. Blend sugar and cinnamon; sprinkle over prunes. Bake 15 minutes. Lightly beat egg yolks and sour cream. Pour over prunes. Return to oven and continue baking 30 minutes. Cool.

CINNAMON SWIRL BREAD

Smells heavenly while baking; tastes even better!

Makes 1 loaf

¼ cup C & H Granulated
    Sugar
1 package active dry
    yeast
½ teaspoon salt
3 to 3½ cups all-purpose
    flour
½ cup milk
¼ cup water

¼ cup (½ stick) butter or
    margarine
1 egg
1 tablespoon butter,
    melted
2 tablespoons C & H
    Granulated Sugar
½ teaspoon cinnamon

Grease 9x5x3-inch loaf pan. In large bowl, mix ¼ cup sugar, the yeast, salt and 1 cup of the flour. Heat milk, water and ¼ cup butter until lukewarm (110°F)—butter will not be melted. Add to flour mixture; beat 1 minute. Add 1 cup additional flour and the egg; beat 2 minutes. With a spoon, stir in 1 to 1½ cups flour until dough holds shape. Turn out onto floured board. Knead 8 minutes or until dough is smooth and elastic (it should not be firm or sticky). Cover with waxed paper and towel. Let rest 20 minutes.

Punch dough down and roll into an 8x15-inch rectangle. Brush with melted butter. Sprinkle with 2 tablespoons sugar and the cinnamon. Starting with narrow end, roll up jelly-roll fashion. Seal ends; place seam side down in loaf pan. Cover pan with plastic wrap; refrigerate 2 to 4 hours.

Before baking, remove wrap; pierce any air bubbles with oiled toothpick. Let stand at room temperature 20 minutes while oven preheats to 350°F. Bake 40 to 45 minutes or until bread sounds hollow when tapped. Turn out onto rack to cool.

GOLDEN KUCHEN

Colonial wives would have recognized this—it's first cousin to their Sally Lunn

Makes 10 to 12 servings

1 package active dry
    yeast
1 cup lukewarm water
    (105° to 115°F)
3¼ cups all-purpose flour
1 cup C & H Granulated
    Sugar

½ cup (1 stick) butter or
    margarine, softened
½ teaspoon EACH salt *and*
    nutmeg
1 tablespoon grated
    lemon rind
4 eggs

Preheat oven to 375°F. Grease and flour 10-inch tube pan or mold. In small bowl, dissolve yeast in warm water; mix in 1 cup of flour. Set in warm place 30 minutes or until bubbly. In large bowl, combine sugar, butter, salt, nutmeg and lemon rind; cream until fluffy. Beat in eggs, 1 at a time. Beat in yeast mixture. Blend in remaining flour, beating at medium-low speed until smooth. Pour into pan, filling it no more than half full. Let rise in warm place until batter is about ¼ inch from top. Bake 50 to 60 minutes or until cake tester inserted in center comes out clean. Cool slightly in pan. Loosen edges with knife tip, then turn out onto rack.

Note: Kuchen may also be baked in two 5-cup tube pans 35 to 40 minutes.

2 BEST-EVER COOKIES

It's impossible to keep a cookie jar full!

Cookies aren't just for Christmas. They're for lunch boxes and afterschool snacks, for afternoon tea or the elegant finishing touch to a rich dessert. And above all, they're for dunking and enjoying. With know-how and the proper equipment, they're a snap to make, particularly drop cookies and rich bar cookies. You'll find recipes for brownies, the most famous of the bar cookies, on pages 148-149.

Flour is the greatest bugaboo of cookie making. No matter what kind of cookie you're preparing, stir the dough as little as possible after adding the flour. Too much stirring and you have a tough cookie on your hands.

Too much flour also produces a tough cookie. Always measure flour sparingly—put as little as possible into each cup. To avoid over-flouring of rolled cookies, roll the dough between sheets of waxed paper or use a pastry cloth and cloth-covered pin for rolling the cookies. Chill the dough 2 to 4 hours for easier handling but do not overchill as the dough will crack. Roll the dough evenly so that the cookies will all be the same thickness and bake evenly. Cut out cookies as close together as possible. Scraps may be rerolled if you have been careful not to get too much flour into the dough, but these cookies will never be as good as those from the first rolling.

Molded cookies may be shaped by hand, but if you are planning to use a cookie press or pastry bag (with a ribbon or $1/2$- to $3/4$-inch open star tube), make a test cookie before adding all the flour. The dough should be soft enough to go through the press or tube but firm enough to hold its shape. With its full complement of flour, any dough for molded cookies can become refrigerator cookies if properly chilled.

Drop cookies may be formed by picking up the dough with one teaspoon and using a second to push the dough onto the cookie sheet. It's much faster, however, to use a pastry bag with a plain ½- to ¾-inch tube.

Cookies brown gently and evenly on shiny cookie sheets that are at least 2 inches less in each direction than the dimensions of your oven. Have four or five sheets on hand as the dough spreads too much if the sheet is not cool.

Parchment liner paper allows you to use ungreased sheets, to lay out the cookies in advance and to remove them in one swift motion from sheet to rack for cooling. Lacking liner paper, have a wide spatula on hand for removing the cookies to a cooling rack.

Best results are achieved if you bake a single sheet of cookies at a time, using the center rack of the oven. If you bake two sheets at once, they should be rotated in the middle of the baking period to insure that the cookies brown evenly. Watch the timing carefully as cookies burn in a matter of seconds.

Store crisp cookies in a loosely covered jar and soft ones in a tightly covered container. Do not mix flavors. All cookies freeze well. Layer them in a freezer-wrap-lined box, separating the layers with additional wrap. Bring the lining wrap over to enclose the cookies, cover the box and freeze. The cookies will retain their good flavor for 6 to 8 weeks. Bar cookies, properly wrapped, can be frozen up to 6 months.

Unbaked dough for some cookies may also be frozen. Freeze dough for drop cookies 2 to 3 months. To use, thaw until just soft enough to spoon onto sheets. Unbaked molded cookies may be frozen on cookie sheets and then packed in boxes and kept frozen 2 to 3 months. Refrigerator cookie dough can be shaped into a roll, wrapped and frozen 2 to 3 months. Use a sawtooth knife to slice while frozen and bake only what you need; small quantities could even be baked in a toaster-oven. Return unused portion to freezer promptly.

Wholesome Oatie (page 32)

WHOLESOME OATIES

Photograph on page 31

Makes 3 dozen

²/₃ cup C & H Dark
   Brown Sugar, packed
½ cup (1 stick) butter,
   softened
1 egg
1 teaspoon vanilla
1 tablespoon milk
1 cup whole wheat flour

½ teaspoon EACH baking
   powder, baking soda
   and salt
1 teaspoon cinnamon
1 cup uncooked quick
   oats
1 package (6 ounces)
   semisweet
   chocolate chips

Preheat oven to 350°F. Grease cookie sheet. Cream sugar, butter, egg, vanilla and milk. Combine flour, baking powder, soda, salt and cinnamon. Add all at once to creamed mixture; beat until smooth. Stir in oats and chocolate chips. Drop by teaspoonfuls 2 inches apart on cookie sheet. Bake 10 minutes (do not overbake). Cool on rack.

CHOCOLATE CHIP COOKIES

Makes about 4 dozen

1 cup C & H Powdered
   Sugar
½ cup (1 stick) butter or
   margarine, softened
1 egg
1 teaspoon vanilla

1¼ cups all-purpose flour
½ teaspoon EACH baking
   soda *and* salt
1 package (6·ounces)
   chocolate chips
½ cup chopped walnuts

Preheat oven to 375°F. Grease cookie sheet. Cream sugar and butter. Stir in egg and vanilla. Combine flour, soda and salt; stir into creamed mixture. Fold in chocolate chips and nuts. Drop by teaspoonfuls onto cookie sheet. Bake 10 to 12 minutes. Cool on rack.

CARAMEL CRUNCH COOKIES

Makes 8 dozen

Caramel Crunch (recipe
follows)
1½ cups C & H Granulated
Sugar
½ cup EACH shortening
and butter,
softened

2 eggs
3 tablespoons cream or
evaporated milk
1 teaspoon vanilla
3 cups all-purpose flour
½ teaspoon EACH baking
soda *and* salt

Prepare Caramel Crunch. Preheat oven to 375°F. Cream sugar, shortening and butter. Beat in eggs, 1 at a time. Add cream and vanilla. Combine flour, soda and salt; mix into dough. Stir in Caramel Crunch. Drop in small mounds on ungreased cookie sheet. Bake 10 to 12 minutes or until lightly browned. Cool on rack.

Caramel Crunch

Grease cookie sheet lightly with butter. In small heavy skillet, melt 1 cup C & H Granulated Sugar over low heat, swirling pan occasionally. Raise heat to medium and cook until sugar becomes a clear golden syrup. Carefully pour a thin layer onto cookie sheet. When cool and hard, break into tiny pieces.

Note: Caramel Crunch is also a delicious topping for ice cream and puddings.

Hint: How should brown sugar be stored? Keep brown sugar purchased in the C & H Clear-Pak in its plastic bag. Once opened, reclose and fasten tightly. Store the cardboard carton in a cool, moist place. After using, refold glassine liner and close box. Or, empty the sugar into a container and keep tightly closed.

PUMPKIN DROP COOKIES

Makes about 5 dozen

1 cup C & H Dark Brown Sugar, packed
¾ cup (1½ sticks) butter or margarine, softened
2 eggs
1 cup cooked or canned pumpkin puree
2 cups all-purpose flour

½ teaspoon EACH baking powder, baking soda, cinnamon *and* nutmeg
¼ teaspoon EACH ground cloves *and* salt
1 cup raisins
½ cup chopped nuts

Preheat oven to 375°F. Grease cookie sheet. Cream sugar and butter. Beat in eggs. Blend in pumpkin. Combine flour, baking powder, soda, cinnamon, nutmeg, cloves and salt; mix into creamed mixture. Stir in raisins and nuts. Drop by teaspoonfuls onto cookie sheet. Bake 12 to 15 minutes or until lightly browned. Cool on rack. Cookies will be soft.

CREAM CHEESE COOKIES

Makes about 4 dozen

1 cup C & H Powdered Sugar
¾ cup (1½ sticks) butter or margarine, softened
1 package (3 ounces) cream cheese, softened
1 teaspoon vanilla

1 tablespoon lemon juice
2 teaspoons grated lemon rind
2 cups cake flour or 1¾ cups all-purpose flour
1 cup minced pecans
C & H Powdered Sugar (for coating)

Preheat oven to 300°F. Gradually beat 1 cup sugar into butter and cream cheese until light and fluffy. Stir in vanilla, lemon juice and rind. Mix in flour, then stir in nuts. Push off teaspoon onto ungreased cookie sheet. Bake 20 to 25 minutes or until lightly browned. While hot, coat with powdered sugar. Cool on rack.

AFTERSCHOOL CARROT COOKIES

Makes 3 dozen

½ cup boiling water
½ cup raisins
1 cup C & H Dark Brown
Sugar, packed
½ cup shortening
1 egg
1 teaspoon lemon extract

½ cup finely shredded
raw carrot
1½ cups all-purpose flour
2 teaspoons baking
powder
½ teaspoon salt

Preheat oven to 400°F. Grease cookie sheet. Pour boiling water over raisins; soak 5 minutes, then drain. Beat sugar, shortening, egg and lemon extract in bowl. Stir in carrot and drained raisins. Combine flour, baking powder and salt; stir into carrot mixture. Drop by teaspoonfuls onto cookie sheet. Bake 10 to 12 minutes. Cool on rack.

ANGEL FOOD COOKIES

Makes 4 dozen

3 egg whites
Pinch EACH salt *and*
cream of tartar
1 cup C & H Granulated
Sugar
½ teaspoon EACH vanilla
and lemon extract

1 cup snipped dates
1 cup coarsely chopped
walnuts
1 cup all-purpose flour

Preheat oven to 350°F. Grease cookie sheet. Beat egg whites with salt and cream of tartar until soft peaks form. Add sugar, 1 tablespoon at a time, and beat until meringue is stiff and glossy. Stir in vanilla and lemon extract. Mix dates, walnuts and flour; fold into meringue. Drop by teaspoonfuls onto cookie sheet. Bake 10 to 12 minutes. Cool on rack.

AMARETTI

Makes about 4 dozen

¾ cup (4 ounces) blanched
almonds, toasted
2 egg whites
¼ teaspoon salt
⅛ teaspoon cream of
tartar

1 cup C & H Golden
Brown Sugar, packed
¼ teaspoon almond
extract

Preheat oven to 350°F. Line cookie sheet with parchment or brown paper. Pulverize almonds in blender or food processor. Beat egg whites with salt and cream of tartar until soft peaks form. Add sugar, 1 tablespoon at a time, and continue beating until meringue is stiff and glossy. Fold in ground almonds and almond extract. Drop by teaspoonfuls 1 inch apart on prepared cookie sheet. Bake 10 to 12 minutes, or until lightly browned. Wait 2 to 3 minutes before transferring to rack to cool.

PRUNE SURPRISE COOKIES

Makes 5 dozen

30 pitted prunes
60 walnut pieces
1 cup C & H Golden
Brown Sugar, packed
½ cup (1 stick) butter or
margarine, softened
1 egg

1½ cups all-purpose flour
½ teaspoon EACH baking
powder *and* baking
soda
¼ teaspoon salt
½ cup sour cream

Preheat oven 400°F. Grease cookie sheet. Cut prunes in half and wrap each around 1 walnut piece; set aside. Cream sugar and butter. Beat in egg. Combine flour, baking powder, soda and salt. Add to creamed mixture alternately with sour cream, beginning and ending with dry ingredients. One at a time, turn stuffed prunes in batter until completely coated. Place on cookie sheet. Bake 9 to 10 minutes. Cool on rack.

FROSTED BUTTERSCOTCH COOKIES

Photograph on page 42

Makes 8 dozen

1½ cups C & H Brown
    Sugar, packed
½ cup shortening
2 eggs
1 teaspoon vanilla
2½ cups all-purpose flour
1 teaspoon baking soda

½ teaspoon EACH baking
    powder *and* salt
½ pint (1 cup) sour cream
½ cup minced nuts
    Golden Butter Frosting
    (recipe follows)

Preheat oven to 400°F. Grease cookie sheet. Cream sugar and shortening. Add eggs and vanilla; mix well. Combine flour, soda, baking powder and salt and add alternately with sour cream; mix well. Stir in nuts. Drop by teaspoonfuls onto cookie sheet. Bake 10 to 12 minutes or until cookies are puffed and lightly browned. When cookies are cool, frost with Golden Butter Frosting.

Golden Butter Frosting

½ cup (1 stick) butter
2 cups C & H Powdered
    Sugar

1 teaspoon vanilla
    Coarsely chopped nuts

Heat butter until golden brown. Blend in sugar and vanilla. Spread on cookies. (If frosting becomes stiff, stir in a few drops of warm water.) Dip frosted top of cookies into nuts.

Hint: Toast slivered or whole blanched almonds on a cookie sheet in a 350°F oven 15 minutes or until golden brown. Stir frequently to avoid burning.

CHOCOLATE MERINGUE PUFFS

Makes 3½ dozen

6 ounces semisweet chocolate

2 egg whites
Pinch of salt

⅛ teaspoon cream of tartar

¾ cup C & H Powdered Sugar

½ teaspoon EACH white vinegar *and* vanilla

½ cup chopped walnuts

Preheat oven to 350°F. Melt chocolate in double boiler over simmering water. Set aside. Beat egg whites with salt and cream of tartar until soft peaks form. Beat in sugar, 1 tablespoon at a time, until stiff and glossy. Beat in vinegar and vanilla. Fold in melted chocolate and nuts. Drop by teaspoonfuls onto ungreased cookie sheet. Bake 10 minutes. Cool on rack.

LACY COOKIE ROLLS

Makes 4 dozen

⅔ cup C & H Golden Brown Sugar, packed

½ cup (1 stick) butter or margarine

½ cup corn syrup

1 cup flour

1 cup minced nuts

Preheat oven to 325°F. Grease cookie sheet. Combine sugar, butter and corn syrup in top of double boiler. Stir over direct medium heat until well blended. Remove from heat and mix in flour and nuts; place over boiling water to keep batter warm while working. Drop by teaspoonfuls onto cookie sheet, leaving 1 inch between cookies. (Stagger batches so they will not all finish baking at the same time.) Bake 10 to 12 minutes until golden brown. Remove cookie sheet from oven and cool 2 minutes. Loosen cookies with spatula one at a time and roll around any clean, round surface (such as the handle of a wooden spoon) until firm. If cookies become too firm to shape, return to oven for several seconds to soften.

Top: Chocolate Meringue Puffs, bottom: Lacy Cookie Rolls

JEAN'S MOLASSES COOKIES

Photograph on page 42

Makes 7 dozen

1 cup C & H Golden
  Brown Sugar, packed
1 cup shortening
1 cup light molasses
1 cup boiling water
4 cups all-purpose flour

2 teaspoons EACH baking
  powder *and* cinnamon
1 teaspoon EACH salt *and*
  baking soda
1 cup chopped nuts
½ cup wheat germ
  (optional)

Preheat oven to 400°F. Grease cookie sheet. Stir sugar and shortening together until well blended. Add molasses, then stir in boiling water. Combine flour, baking powder, cinnamon, salt and soda. Stir into sugar mixture along with nuts and wheat germ; mix well. Chill until firm. Drop by small teaspoonfuls onto cookie sheet and bake 8 to 10 minutes until soft and puffy. Do not overbake. Cool on rack.

CHINESE CHEWS

A favorite at C & H company luncheons

Makes about 3 dozen

4 tablespoons C & H
  Brown Sugar
½ cup (1 stick) butter or
  margarine, softened
2 cups all-purpose flour
⅛ teaspoon salt

3 cups C & H Golden
  Brown Sugar, packed
1½ cups chopped nuts
1½ cups flaked coconut
4 eggs, beaten
4 teaspoons vanilla

Preheat oven to 350°F. Grease 13x9-inch pan. Blend 4 tablespoons brown sugar, the butter, flour and salt with pastry blender. Turn mixture into pan and pat until firm. Bake 20 minutes. Combine remaining ingredients, spread in pan and return to oven 30 minutes longer or until center is firm. Cool in pan. Cut into bars.

WAIKIKI BANANA BARS

No eggs needed in these moist chewy bars

Makes about 1½ dozen

1 cup C & H Golden Brown Sugar, packed	½ teaspoon salt
¼ cup shortening	1 cup mashed ripe bananas (2 to 3 medium)
½ teaspoon vanilla	
½ teaspoon lemon extract	½ cup chopped nuts
1½ cups all-purpose flour	2 tablespoons C & H Powdered Sugar
1½ teaspoons baking powder	1 teaspoon cinnamon

Preheat oven to 350°F. Grease 11x7-inch pan. Cream brown sugar and shortening; blend in vanilla and lemon extract. Combine flour, baking powder and salt. Stir into creamed mixture alternately with bananas, mixing well after each addition. Stir in nuts. Pour into pan. Bake 30 to 35 minutes. Blend powdered sugar and cinnamon; sift over top. Cool in pan. Cut into bars.

APPLE BARS

Makes about 2½ dozen small bars

1 cup C & H Golden Brown Sugar, packed	1 teaspoon EACH baking soda *and* cinnamon
¼ cup (½ stick) butter or margarine, softened	½ teaspoon nutmeg
	¼ teaspoon salt
1 egg	½ cup chopped nuts
2 cups chopped unpeeled apples	⅓ cup raisins (optional)
1 cup all-purpose flour	1 cup C & H Powdered Sugar

Preheat oven to 350°F. Grease 9-inch square pan. Cream brown sugar, butter and egg until light and fluffy. Stir in apples. Combine flour, soda, cinnamon, nutmeg and salt and stir into apple mixture. Mix in nuts and raisins. Spread batter (it will be stiff) evenly in pan. Bake 40 to 45 minutes. Cool in pan. Cut into bars and coat with powdered sugar.

MARZIPAN BARS

Makes 3 dozen

2½ cups C & H Powdered
   Sugar
1½ cups ground blanched
   almonds
1 egg white
2 tablespoons water
2 cups all-purpose flour

2 teaspoons baking
   powder
1 cup (2 sticks) butter or
   margarine, softened
1 egg
½ teaspoon vanilla

Preheat oven to 350°F. Grease 13x9-inch pan. Blend 2 cups sugar and the almonds. Stir in egg white and water; set aside.

Combine ½ cup sugar, the flour and baking powder. Cut butter into dry ingredients with pastry blender or fingertips until mixture resembles coarse meal. Stir in egg and vanilla. Set aside ¾ cup dough. Press remaining dough evenly into pan. Spread marzipan (almond mixture) over dough. Shape remaining dough into strips and arrange in open lattice pattern over filling. Bake 35 minutes. Cool completely before cutting into bars.

Counter-clockwise on table: Frosted Butterscotch Cookies with Golden Butter Frosting (page 37), Anise Cookie Slices (page 57), Fudge Strata Cookies (page 58), Glazed Brown Sugar Bars (page 45), Jean's Molasses Cookies (page 40), Marzipan Bars. On plate: Chewy Cocoa Bars (page 47) and Golden Thumbprints (page 56).

APRICOT BARS

Makes about 2½ dozen

1 cup snipped dried
    apricots
¾ cup water
1½ cups C & H Golden
    Brown Sugar, packed
1 cup all-purpose flour
6 tablespoons (¾ stick)
    butter or margarine
1 tablespoon cornstarch

¼ teaspoon salt
1 cup coarsely chopped
    nuts
2 eggs
2 tablespoons orange
    juice
2 teaspoons grated
    orange rind

Preheat oven to 350°F. Grease 11x7-inch or 9-inch square pan. Combine apricots and water in small saucepan. Simmer, covered, 20 minutes. Meanwhile, combine ½ cup of the sugar, the flour and butter; mix with pastry blender or fingertips until crumbly. Press into pan. Bake 20 minutes.

While crust bakes, mix remaining 1 cup sugar with cornstarch and salt; stir into undrained apricots and cook until thickened, stirring constantly. Remove from heat; stir in nuts, eggs, orange juice and rind. Spread apricot mixture over baked crust. Bake 25 minutes. Cool in pan; cut into bars.

 # MACADAMIA NUT BARS

Makes about 3½ dozen

1 cup C & H Granulated
    Sugar
1 cup (2 sticks) butter,
    softened
1 egg
1 teaspoon vanilla

2 cups all-purpose flour
1½ cups (7 ounces)
    chopped macadamia
    nuts, almonds or
    hazelnuts

Preheat oven to 350°F. Grease 13x9-inch baking pan. Cream sugar and butter. Beat in egg and vanilla. Blend in flour. Stir in half the nuts. Spread batter (it will be thick) evenly in pan. Sprinkle remaining nuts over batter. Bake 25 to 30 minutes. While hot, cut into bars; transfer to rack to cool.

GLAZED BROWN SUGAR BARS

Photograph on page 42

Makes 2½ dozen

2 cups C & H Golden
   Brown sugar, packed
½ cup (1 stick) butter or
   margarine, softened
2 teaspoons vanilla
2 eggs (1 separated)
2 cups all-purpose flour

1 teaspoon baking powder
¼ teaspoon salt
1 cup coarsely chopped
   nuts
   Pinch EACH salt *and*
   cream of tartar
½ cup finely chopped nuts

Preheat oven to 350°F. Grease 13 x 9-inch pan. Cream 1 cup sugar and the butter. Beat in 1 teaspoon vanilla, 1 egg and 1 egg yolk (reserve egg white). Combine flour, baking powder and salt. Stir into creamed mixture along with 1 cup coarse nuts. Spread evenly in pan. Beat reserved egg white with salt and cream of tartar until stiff. Beat in remaining 1 cup sugar and 1 teaspoon vanilla until completely mixed; stir in ½ cup fine nuts. Spread over top of dough. Bake 30 minutes. Cool in pan 10 minutes, then cut into bars and finish cooling on rack.

ALMOND TOFFEE BARS

Makes 3 dozen

1 cup C & H Golden
   Brown Sugar, packed
1 cup (2 sticks) butter or
   margarine, softened
1 egg yolk
1 teaspoon vanilla

2¼ cups cake flour
   (or 2 cups
   all-purpose flour
   less ½ tablespoon)
9 to 10 ounces milk
   chocolate pieces
½ cup chopped almonds

Preheat oven to 350°F. Cream sugar, butter, egg yolk and vanilla. Stir in flour. Spread batter evenly in 15x10-inch pan. Bake 20 minutes. Immediately sprinkle chocolate pieces over baked layer. Wait 3 to 5 minutes until chocolate melts, then spread evenly with spatula. Sprinkle with nuts, pressing them lightly into warm chocolate. Cool in pan; cut into bars.

CRUNCHY LEMON BARS

Makes 1 1/2 dozen

1 1/2 cups C & H Powdered
   Sugar
1/2 cup (1 stick) butter or
   margarine, softened
2 eggs, separated
1 cup all-purpose flour
1/4 teaspoon salt

2 teaspoons grated lemon
   rind
2 tablespoons lemon juice
   Pinch EACH salt *and*
   cream of tartar
1/2 cup chopped nuts

Preheat oven to 350°F. Cream 1/2 cup sugar and the butter. Stir in egg yolks, then add flour, 1/4 teaspoon salt, the lemon rind and 1 tablespoon lemon juice. Spread batter (it will be stiff) in ungreased 9-inch square pan. Bake 10 minutes.

While crust is baking, beat egg whites with pinch salt and cream of tartar until soft peaks form. Gradually beat in 1 cup sugar, 1 tablespoon at a time; continue beating until stiff peaks form. Stir in 1 tablespoon lemon juice. Fold in nuts. Spread topping evenly over baked crust. Return to oven and continue baking 25 minutes. Cool in pan slightly. Cut into bars.

CALIFORNIA GOLD BARS

Makes about 2 1/2 dozen

1 cup C & H Golden
   Brown Sugar, packed
1 cup (2 sticks) butter or
   margarine, softened
1 egg

1 teaspoon vanilla
1 3/4 cups all-purpose flour
1 cup chopped walnuts or
   macadamia nuts
1/2 cup apricot jam

Preheat oven to 325°F. Grease 9-inch square pan. Cream sugar, butter, egg and vanilla. Stir in flour and nuts. Spoon half the batter evenly into pan. Spread jam over batter. Top jam with remaining batter. Bake 50 minutes. Cool 10 minutes. Cut into bars.

CHEWY COCOA BARS

Photograph on page 42

Makes 2 dozen

¾ cup C & H Powdered
   Sugar
6 tablespoons (¾ stick)
   butter or margarine,
   softened
1 cup all-purpose flour
1 tablespoon milk
1 cup C & H Granulated
   Sugar
½ cup cocoa powder

2 tablespoons flour
½ teaspoon EACH baking
   powder *and* salt
2 eggs, lightly beaten
1 teaspoon vanilla
¼ teaspoon almond
   extract (optional)
1 cup chopped almonds or
   pecans

Preheat oven to 350°F. Cream powdered sugar and butter. Blend in 1 cup flour and the milk. Spread batter evenly on bottom of ungreased 9-inch square pan. Bake 10 minutes.

While crust is baking, combine granulated sugar, cocoa, 2 table-spoons flour, the baking powder and salt in bowl. Beat in eggs, vanilla and almond extract; fold in nuts. Spread topping on baked crust. Return to oven and continue baking about 15 minutes or until top is no longer shiny. While warm, cut into bars.

CRISP SUGAR COOKIES

Makes 6 dozen

1½ cups C & H Granulated
   Sugar
½ cup shortening
½ cup (1 stick) butter or
   margarine, softened
2 eggs
3 tablespoons sweet or
   sour cream

1 teaspoon vanilla
3 cups all-purpose flour
½ teaspoon EACH baking
   soda *and* salt
   C & H Granulated
   Sugar

Gradually beat sugar into shortening and butter, creaming until fluffy. Beat in eggs, 1 at a time. Stir in cream and vanilla. Combine flour, soda and salt. Stir into creamed mixture. Chill 2 hours or overnight.

Preheat oven to 400°F. On lightly floured board, roll half the dough to ⅛-inch thickness. (Leave reserved dough in refrigerator until ready to roll.) Cut shapes with various cookie cutters. Place on ungreased cookie sheet. Sprinkle with sugar. Repeat with other half of dough. Bake 6 to 9 minutes. Cool on rack.

SHORTBREAD COOKIES

Long, slow baking makes these cookies crisp and short (flaky)

Makes about 3 dozen

½ cup C & H Powdered
   Sugar
½ cup (1 stick) butter or
   margarine, softened
1 egg

1½ cups all-purpose flour
½ teaspoon baking powder
   C & H Powdered Sugar
   (for coating; optional)

Cream ½ cup sugar and the butter. Beat in egg, then stir in flour and baking powder. Knead until dough is shiny. Chill 30 minutes.

Preheat oven to 325°F. Roll dough to ½-inch thickness and cut with star or other cookie cutter. Prick with fork. Bake on ungreased cookie sheet 25 to 30 minutes or until light straw color. If desired, coat cookies with sugar immediately; when cool, coat again.

FROSTED GINGERBREAD COOKIES

Ready to roll as soon as it is mixed, this sturdy dough is easy for children to handle

Makes about 3 dozen

¾ cup C & H Dark Brown Sugar, packed
½ cup shortening
½ cup molasses
1 egg
3 cups all-purpose flour
2 teaspoons baking powder

½ teaspoon EACH salt, ground ginger *and* cinnamon
¼ teaspoon ground cloves
Decorator's Frosting (recipe follows)

Preheat oven to 350°F. Grease cookie sheet. Cream sugar and shortening. Beat in molasses and egg. Combine flour, baking powder, salt, ginger, cinnamon and cloves. Stir into creamed mixture and mix until firm. Roll dough to ⅛-inch thickness on floured board. Cut into desired shapes with cookie cutters. Place on cookie sheet. Bake 10 to 12 minutes. Cool on rack. Decorate with Decorator's Frosting.

Decorator's Frosting

2 cups C & H Powdered Sugar
2 tablespoons butter or margarine, softened

1 egg white
Pinch of salt
½ teaspoon vanilla
Food coloring (optional)

Combine all ingredients and beat until smooth. If too thin, add additional powdered sugar. If too thick, add drops of milk or water.

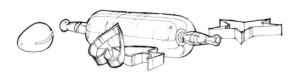

CRISP CUTOUTS

Crisp Cutouts are fun to make at any time of the year but add a particularly festive note to holidays

Makes 5 dozen

1 cup C & H Granulated Sugar
1 cup shortening (or ½ cup [1 stick] butter, softened, and ½ cup shortening)
2 eggs
1 teaspoon vanilla
½ teaspoon almond extract

3½ cups all-purpose flour
1 teaspoon salt
½ teaspoon baking powder
Candied fruits, sprinkles and colored sugar (optional decorations)
Frosting (optional)

Gradually beat sugar into shortening, creaming well. Mix in eggs, 1 at a time, beating well after each addition. Add vanilla and almond extract. Mix flour, salt and baking powder and stir into creamed mixture. Chill dough at least 30 minutes for ease in handling.

Preheat oven to 375°F. Roll dough to ⅛-inch thickness on lightly floured board. Cut shapes with cookie cutters or trace around pattern with knife. If cookies are to be hung for decoration, pierce small hole in dough ½ inch from top edge. Bake on ungreased cookie sheet 8 to 10 minutes until lightly browned. Cool on rack.

To decorate cookies: Decorate with candied fruits, sprinkles or colored sugar before baking or bake without decorations and frost or decorate afterwards.

Crisp Cutouts

RICH
PEANUT BUTTER COOKIES

Makes about 6 dozen

½ cup C & H Granulated
 Sugar
½ cup C & H Dark Brown
 Sugar, packed
¼ cup shortening
¼ cup (½ stick) butter,
 softened

½ cup peanut butter
2 eggs
1½ cups all-purpose flour
½ teaspoon EACH baking
 powder, baking soda
 and salt

Grease cookie sheet. Cream sugars, shortening, butter and peanut butter until fluffy. Beat in eggs, 1 at a time. Combine flour, baking powder, soda and salt and stir into sugar mixture. Chill dough 30 minutes.

Preheat oven to 350°F. With floured hands, shape dough into 1-inch balls. Place on cookie sheet and flatten with floured fork. Bake 8 to 10 minutes. Cool on rack.

CHOCOLATE PEANUT BUTTER
COOKIES

Makes about 6 dozen

1½ cups C & H Golden
 Brown Sugar, packed
½ cup (1 stick) butter,
 softened
2 eggs
1½ teaspoons vanilla
½ cup peanut butter

⅓ cup milk
2 cups all-purpose flour
½ cup cocoa powder
2 teaspoons baking
 powder
½ teaspoon salt

Preheat oven to 400°F. Grease cookie sheet. Cream sugar, butter, eggs and vanilla. Beat in peanut butter and milk, then mix in flour, cocoa, baking powder and salt. Shape into small balls. Place on cookie sheet and flatten with a fork. Bake 8 to 10 minutes. Cool on rack.

GINGERSNAPS

Makes 4 dozen

1 cup C & H Dark Brown
  Sugar, packed
3/4 cup shortening
1 egg
1/4 cup molasses
2 cups all-purpose flour
2 teaspoons baking soda

1 teaspoon EACH ground
  ginger, cinnamon
  and ground cloves
1/4 teaspoon salt
  C & H Granulated
  Sugar

Grease cookie sheet. Cream brown sugar, shortening and egg. Stir in molasses. Combine flour, soda, ginger, cinnamon, cloves and salt. Stir into creamed mixture. Chill dough 30 minutes.

Preheat oven to 350°F. Shape dough into 1-inch balls and roll in granulated sugar. Place 2 inches apart on cookie sheet. Bake 12 to 15 minutes. Cool on rack.

COCONUT CRISPIES

Makes 5 dozen

1 cup C & H Granulated
  Sugar
1/2 cup (1 stick) butter or
  margarine, softened
1 egg
2 teaspoons vanilla
1 cup flaked coconut

1½ cups all-purpose flour
1½ teaspoons baking
  powder
1/4 teaspoon salt
  C & H Granulated
  Sugar

Lightly grease cookie sheet. Cream sugar, butter, egg and vanilla. Stir in coconut. Combine flour, baking powder and salt; blend into coconut mixture. Chill dough 30 minutes.

Preheat oven to 400°F. Shape dough into 1-inch balls and place 2 inches apart on cookie sheet. Press flat with bottom of glass that has been dipped in sugar. Bake 8 to 10 minutes. Cool on rack.

PECAN COOKIE BALLS

Makes about 5 dozen

¼ cup C & H Powdered
  Sugar
½ cup (1 stick) butter or
  margarine, softened
1 teaspoon vanilla

1 cup all-purpose flour
  Pinch of salt
1 cup minced pecans
  C & H Powdered Sugar
  (for coating)

Cream ¼ cup sugar and the butter. Add vanilla. Stir in flour, salt and nuts. Chill dough, if convenient.

Preheat oven to 350°F. Grease cookie sheet. Shape dough into ¾-inch balls (size of large marbles). Place on cookie sheet. Bake 15 minutes or until creamy tan in color. Immediately roll hot cookies in sugar. Cool on rack, then roll again in sugar.

CHOCOLATE DAINTIES

Makes 3 dozen

1 cup C & H Powdered
  Sugar
1 cup (2 sticks) butter or
  margarine, softened
1 teaspoon vanilla

1 tablespoon water
2¼ cups all-purpose flour
¼ cup cocoa powder
1 cup minced nuts
  C & H Powdered Sugar

Preheat oven to 300°F. Cream sugar and butter until light and fluffy. Add vanilla and water. Combine flour and cocoa; stir into creamed mixture along with nuts. Roll dough into small logs about 2 inches long and ¾ inch in diameter (about the size of cocktail franks). Bake on ungreased cookie sheet 20 minutes. While hot, roll cookies in powdered sugar; cool, then roll in powdered sugar again.

SESAME PEARL COOKIES

Makes about 3 dozen

½ cup C & H Golden
   Brown Sugar, packed
¾ cup (1½ sticks) butter or
   margarine, softened
½ teaspoon vanilla

1½ cups all-purpose flour
   Pinch of salt
5 to 6 tablespoons sesame
   seeds

Preheat oven to 325°F. Cream sugar, butter and vanilla. Beat in flour and salt. Shape into 1-inch balls and roll in sesame seeds. Place 2 inches apart on ungreased cookie sheet. Bake 20 minutes. Cool on rack until firm.

HEDDA'S COOKIES

Makes about 5 dozen

1 cup C & H Granulated
   Sugar
1 cup shortening
1 egg
1 teaspoon almond
   extract

1½ cups all-purpose flour
½ teaspoon salt
2 cups flaked coconut

Preheat oven to 325°F. Cream sugar, shortening, egg and almond extract. Mix in flour and salt. Stir in coconut. Shape into 1-inch balls. Place on ungreased cookie sheet. Flatten with fork. Bake 15 to 18 minutes, until slightly golden around edges. Cool on rack.

Hint: Cookies made with C & H Powdered Sugar are wonderfully light and delicate. Be sure to measure the sugar directly from the box—it's not necessary to sift for these recipes.

GOLDEN THUMBPRINTS

Photograph on page 42

Makes 2½ dozen

⅓ cup C & H Golden Brown Sugar, packed
½ cup (1 stick) butter or margarine, softened
1 egg, separated
½ teaspoon vanilla
1 cup all-purpose flour
¼ teaspoon salt
¾ cup minced walnuts
Candied cherries, jelly or melted semisweet chocolate

Preheat oven to 375°F. Cream sugar, butter, egg yolk and vanilla. Stir in flour and salt. Roll dough into 1-inch balls. Dip into slightly beaten egg white and roll in nuts. Place on ungreased cookie sheet. Bake 5 minutes. Remove from oven. Quickly indent each cookie center with thumb. Return to oven and bake 8 more minutes. Cool on rack. Fill each thumbprint with half a candied cherry, a bit of jelly or melted chocolate.

PINWHEEL COOKIES

Makes 5 dozen

1 cup C & H Powdered Sugar
½ cup (1 stick) butter or margarine, softened
1 egg
1 teaspoon vanilla
1½ cups all-purpose flour
¼ teaspoon EACH baking powder *and* salt
1 ounce unsweetened chocolate, melted

Cream sugar and butter. Beat in egg and vanilla. Mix in flour, baking powder and salt. Divide dough in half. Mix melted chocolate into one half. Chill both halves 30 minutes, or until firm enough to roll. Roll each half into a 6x16-inch rectangle between 2 sheets of waxed paper. Remove waxed paper from 1 side of each piece. Place chocolate dough over white dough and press together, sealing lightly with rolling pin. Remove paper from chocolate dough. Roll up lengthwise, and wrap in waxed paper. Chill overnight.

Preheat oven to 350°F. Cut roll into ¼-inch slices and arrange on ungreased cookie sheet. Bake 10 minutes. Cool on rack.

SUNFLOWER COOKIES

Makes about 3 dozen

¾ cup C & H Golden
　　Brown Sugar, packed
1 cup (2 sticks) butter or
　　margarine, softened
1 egg
1½ cups whole wheat flour
1 cup wheat germ

½ cup roasted sunflower
　　seeds
½ cup carob chips or
　　semisweet chocolate
　　chips
C & H Granulated
　　Sugar

Preheat oven to 350°F. Cream sugar and butter until light and fluffy. Mix in egg, flour, wheat germ, sunflower seeds and carob chips. Shape into 1½-inch balls. Place on ungreased cookie sheet. Flatten to ¼-inch thickness with glass that has been dipped in sugar. Bake 10 minutes or until lightly browned. Cool on rack.

ANISE COOKIE SLICES

Photograph on page 42

Makes 4 dozen

1½ cups C & H Powdered
　　Sugar
½ cup (1 stick) butter or
　　margarine, softened
1 package (3 ounces)
　　cream cheese,
　　softened

4 eggs
3¼ cups all-purpose flour
1 tablespoon baking
　　powder
½ teaspoon salt
2 teaspoons anise seeds

Cream sugar, butter and cream cheese. Add eggs, 1 at a time, beating well after each addition. (Mixture may look curdled.) Add remaining ingredients; mix well. Chill dough 3 hours.

Preheat oven to 350°F. Divide dough in half. On a 17x14-inch cookie sheet, shape each half into a log 1½ inches wide and 17 inches long (the length of the cookie sheet). Bake 30 to 35 minutes. Remove from oven and cut logs into ¾-inch-wide slices. Place on cookie sheet, cut side down, return to oven and bake 10 minutes or until toasted and crisp.

FUDGE STRATA COOKIES

Photograph on page 42

Makes 3 to 4 dozen

6 ounces semisweet chocolate	1 cup (2 sticks) butter or margarine, softened
1½ cups C & H Powdered Sugar	2 teaspoons vanilla
¾ cup chopped walnuts or pecans	2¼ cups cake flour (or 2¼ cups all-purpose flour less 2½ tablespoons)

Melt chocolate in double boiler over simmering water. Stir in ½ cup sugar and the nuts. Spread into a 4x12-inch rectangle on foil or waxed paper; chill.

Gradually beat 1 cup sugar into butter, creaming well. Add vanilla and flour and beat until smooth. Divide dough in half and shape each half into a 2x12-inch bar. Chill.

Cut chilled chocolate into 6 lengthwise strips. Cut each dough bar into 4 lengthwise strips. On foil or waxed paper make 2 striped bars, using 4 cookie strips and 3 chocolate strips in each bar. Press together; wrap and chill.

Preheat oven to 350°F. When ready to bake, remove wrap; cut chilled dough into ½-inch-wide sticks. Bake on ungreased cookie sheet 15 minutes until lightly browned. Handle finished cookies gently.

Hint: Mailing cookies for Christmas or to an away-from-home child? Bar and drop cookies are a good bet. They're less apt to crumble than rolled cookies, which are fragile and could arrive in a shattered state. Moist cookies will also travel better than dry ones.

3 DOWN-HOME FAVORITES

Remember the mouth-watering aromas
of Grandma's kitchen?

Delicious puddings, pies and cakes—these are the homey favorites we remember from childhood. Try one of these heirloom recipes today and recreate that feeling of warmth and family love.

Puddings, custards and pie fillings that contain eggs need coddling. Eggs, like most baking ingredients, should always be at room temperature before using. When preparing puddings and custards on top of the stove, use a double boiler or heavy-bottomed pan over low heat and stir constantly until the mixture is thickened. Don't boil; it will cause curdling. When baking, set the mixture in a pan of water to insure an even flow of tempered heat. Too high a heat will cause "weeping" and cracking. Easy does it is the key.

Grandma excelled in making flaky, rich pie crusts and you can too. Have your shortening and water ice cold (an exception to the room temperature rule!). Add water sparingly to reach the desired consistency. Too much water or too much handling will produce a tough crust. We've provided recipes for two basic pie crusts in this chapter. Neophytes—and those with busy schedules—will love the ease and simplicity of our No-Fail crust. Purists and experimenters will be intrigued by our unusual Butter Crust (powdered sugar in a pie crust?) Try them both, and don't forget to check the index for other classic and not-so-classic crustings.

When you divide pie dough, make the portion for the bottom crust slightly larger than the portion for the top. A bottom crust should roll out 1½ to 2 inches larger than your pie pan; the top crust should roll out 1 inch wider. If practical, chill dough for several hours before rolling. Even a brief 10 minutes in the refrigerator will make the dough easier to handle. Use a pastry cloth and cloth-covered rolling pin to prevent the dough from sticking and tearing. If patches are needed, moisten the edges and press together.

Rolled out dough may be transferred to the pie pan by rolling it around the pin and unrolling it over the pan, or by folding the dough into quarters and gently easing it into the pan, pressing it against the sides and bottom.

Leftover dough can become a special treat for youngsters. Roll out the scraps, spread with soft butter, sprinkle with C and H Brown Sugar, nutmeg and minced nuts. Roll up, cut into thin slices and bake at 425°F until crisp.

Unlike cakes, which are best baked in shiny pans, undercrusts of pies brown better in pans that absorb heat. You'll get good browning with oven glass, enamelware, dull-finish aluminum, stainless steel or darkened tin pans.

The easiest way to keep berry or cherry pies from running over in the oven is to use a lattice top with a high fluted rim. All double-crust pies will have an added sparkle and brown beautifully if you brush the top crust with milk and sprinkle generously with C and H Granulated Sugar before baking.

Unbaked pastry may be frozen in foil pie pans for quick use. To avoid soggy bottoms, filled pies should be baked before freezing. To use, unwrap and let stand 30 minutes. Heat in a 350°F oven until just warm. Custard, cream and meringue-topped pies do not freeze well.

Lemon Puff Pudding (page 62)

LEMON PUFF PUDDING

Photograph on page 61

Makes 6 servings

1 cup C & H Granulated
  Sugar
¼ cup all-purpose flour
3 tablespoons butter or
  margarine, softened
3 eggs, separated
2 teaspoons grated lemon
  rind

¼ cup lemon juice
1½ cups milk
¼ teaspoon salt
⅛ teaspoon cream of
  tartar
Whipped cream
  (optional)

Preheat oven to 325°F. Grease 1½-quart baking dish. Cream half the sugar, the flour and butter. Stir in egg yolks, lemon rind, lemon juice and milk. Beat egg whites with salt and cream of tartar until soft peaks form. Beat in remaining ½ cup sugar, 1 tablespoon at a time, and continue beating until egg whites are stiff but not dry. Fold in creamed mixture. Pour into dish; set dish into larger pan containing enough boiling water to reach halfway up its sides. Bake 1 hour. Cool. If desired, serve with whipped cream.

SCOTCH RICE PUDDING

Dark brown sugar adds old-style flavor

Makes 6 servings

2 cups water
½ teaspoon salt
1 cup uncooked rice
⅔ cup C & H Dark Brown
  Sugar, packed
1 teaspoon vanilla

½ cup whipping or light
  cream
2 tablespoons butter or
  margarine
Cream or vanilla ice
  cream

Bring water to boil. Add salt and slowly stir in rice. Cover pan and cook over low heat 25 to 30 minutes or until liquid is absorbed. Gently stir in sugar, vanilla, ½ cup cream and butter. Serve immediately with cream.

TAPIOCA FRUIT DESSERT

Makes 6 to 8 servings

2 cups milk
2 tablespoons
   quick-cooking tapioca
1/3 cup C & H Granulated
   Sugar
1/4 teaspoon salt
2 eggs, separated

1 teaspoon grated orange
   rind
1/2 teaspoon vanilla
Pinch EACH salt *and*
   cream of tartar
Sweetened strawberries,
   apricots or peaches

Scald 1 1/2 cups of the milk in top of double boiler. Combine tapioca, sugar and 1/4 teaspoon salt; stir into hot milk. Cook, stirring frequently, about 5 minutes or until tapioca is clear. Beat egg yolks with remaining 1/2 cup milk. Stir into tapioca and cook 4 minutes, stirring constantly. Remove from heat. Add orange rind and vanilla. Beat egg whites with pinch salt and cream of tartar until stiff peaks form. Fold into hot tapioca. Cool, then chill. Serve with sweetened fruit.

BREAD-AND-BUTTER PUDDING

Makes 6 servings

5 slices bread
   Butter or margarine,
      softened
1/4 cup raisins
3 eggs
2 1/2 cups milk

3/4 cup C & H Golden
   Brown Sugar, packed
1/2 teaspoon vanilla
Pinch of salt
Nutmeg

Preheat oven to 350°F. Toast bread slices. Spread with butter and cut into cubes. Measure 3 cups cubes and layer with raisins in a 1 1/2-quart casserole. Set aside. Beat eggs; stir in milk, sugar, vanilla and salt. Pour over bread. Soak 30 minutes. Sprinkle with nutmeg. Place casserole in shallow pan filled with enough hot water to reach 1 inch up sides of casserole. Bake 45 to 60 minutes or until custard is set. Serve warm or cold.

BAKED APPLE PUDDING

A warm pudding that will make a winter night seem less cold

Makes 8 servings

1 cup C & H Granulated
    Sugar
¼ cup (½ stick) butter or
    margarine, softened
1 egg
2 cups unpeeled, finely
    shredded apples (2 or
    3 medium)

1 cup all-purpose flour
1 teaspoon EACH baking
    soda *and* cinnamon
¾ teaspoon nutmeg
¼ teaspoon salt
    Vanilla Sauce (recipe
    follows) or sweetened
    whipped cream

Preheat oven to 350°F. Grease 8-inch square pan. Cream sugar and butter until light and fluffy. Beat in egg. Stir in apples, flour, soda, cinnamon, nutmeg and salt. Pour into pan. Bake 45 minutes. Serve warm with Vanilla Sauce or whipped cream.

Vanilla Sauce

1 cup C & H Granulated
    Sugar
½ cup milk
½ cup (1 stick) butter or
    margarine

1 teaspoon vanilla
⅛ teaspoon nutmeg

Stir sugar, milk and butter together over low heat; do not boil! When slightly thickened, stir in vanilla and nutmeg. Serve warm.

CLASSIC CARROT PUDDING

Makes 8 servings

³/₄ cup raisins
¼ cup orange juice
³/₄ cup C & H Golden
    Brown Sugar, packed
½ cup (1 stick) butter or
    margarine, softened
2 eggs
1 cup finely shredded raw
    carrots
1½ cups all-purpose flour

1 teaspoon EACH baking
    powder *and* baking
    soda
½ teaspoon EACH
    cinnamon *and*
    nutmeg
¼ teaspoon salt
    Hard Sauce (recipe
    follows)

Preheat oven to 325°F. Grease and flour 5-cup mold. Soak raisins in orange juice. Cream sugar and butter. Beat in eggs. Stir in carrots. Combine flour, baking powder, soda, cinnamon, nutmeg and salt. Add half the dry ingredients to the carrot mixture. Stir in raisins and orange juice, then add remaining dry ingredients. Mix well. Spoon into mold. Bake 50 to 60 minutes. Unmold and cool on rack. Serve with Hard Sauce.

Hard Sauce

2 cups C & H Powdered
    Sugar

½ cup (1 stick) butter or
    margarine, softened
2 teaspoons vanilla

Cream sugar and butter until light and fluffy. Stir in vanilla and beat until smooth. Chill.

BAKED CRANBERRY PUDDING

*Cranberries are so good it is a shame to confine them to
Thanksgiving and Christmas*

Makes 8 servings

1 cup C & H Granulated
　Sugar
2 cups all-purpose flour
2½ teaspoons baking
　powder
½ teaspoon salt
⅔ cup milk

3 tablespoons butter or
　margarine, melted
1 egg
2 cups raw cranberries
　Buttercream Sauce
　(recipe follows)

Preheat oven to 350°F. Grease 9-inch square pan. Combine sugar,
flour, baking powder and salt. Stir in milk, butter and egg; beat 2
minutes. Stir in cranberries. Pour into pan. Bake 40 minutes. Serve
hot with Buttercream Sauce.

Buttercream Sauce

1½ cups C & H Granulated
　Sugar
¾ cup whipping cream
¼ cup (½ stick) butter

2 egg yolks, slightly
　beaten
1 teaspoon vanilla

Combine sugar, cream and butter in saucepan. Cook over medium
heat, 5 minutes, stirring constantly. Gradually stir hot mixture into
beaten egg yolks, then return to saucepan and stir over low heat
until thickened and smooth. Stir in vanilla. Serve warm.

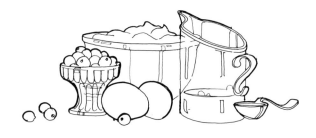

FRESH APPLE CAKE

A spicy cake with a rich brown sugar taste

Makes 12 servings

2 cups C & H Golden
   Brown Sugar, packed
1 cup (2 sticks) butter or
   margarine, softened
4 eggs
2½ cups all-purpose flour
1 teaspoon EACH
   allspice, cinnamon
   and baking soda

½ cup water
2 cups coarsely chopped
   tart baking apples
   (2 to 3 medium)
1 cup minced walnuts
1 teaspoon vanilla
   White Fudge Frosting
   (recipe follows)

Preheat oven to 350°F. Grease and flour 13x9-inch pan. Cream sugar and butter. Add eggs, 1 at a time, beating well after each addition. Combine flour, allspice, cinnamon and soda. Add to creamed mixture alternately with water, beginning and ending with dry ingredients. Fold in apples, walnuts and vanilla. Pour into pan. Bake 45 minutes or until cake tester inserted in center comes out clean. Cool in pan. Frost with White Fudge Frosting.

White Fudge Frosting

¼ cup water
2 tablespoons butter

3 cups C & H Powdered
   Sugar
½ teaspoon vanilla

Heat water and butter in small saucepan until butter melts. Remove from heat and gradually blend in powdered sugar. Add vanilla and beat until smooth.

This frosting can be stored in the refrigerator and thinned with cream as needed.

YOGURT POUND CAKE

Yogurt Pound Cake has a fine-grained texture and a rich flavor emphasized by Apricot Yogurt Frosting

Makes 12 servings

3 cups C & H Golden
  Brown Sugar, packed
1 cup (2 sticks) butter or
  margarine, softened
6 eggs
3 cups all-purpose flour
1/4 teaspoon baking soda

1/2 teaspoon salt
1/2 pint (1 cup) plain yogurt
2 teaspoons vanilla
1/3 cup poppy seeds
  Apricot Yogurt Frosting
  (recipe follows)

Preheat oven to 325°F. Grease and flour 10-inch tube pan. Cream sugar and butter until light and fluffy. Add eggs, 1 at a time, beating well after each addition. Combine flour, soda and salt. Add alternately with yogurt to creamed mixture, beginning and ending with dry ingredients. Stir in vanilla and poppy seeds. Pour into pan. Bake 90 minutes or until cake tester inserted in center comes out clean. Cool 10 minutes in pan, then turn out onto rack to finish cooling. Frost with Apricot Yogurt Frosting.

Apricot Yogurt Frosting

4 cups C & H Powdered
  Sugar
1/4 cup apricot preserves
1/4 cup plain yogurt

1/4 cup (1/2 stick) butter or
  margarine, softened
  Pinch of salt

Combine all ingredients in bowl. Beat until smooth and creamy. Enough to frost two 8- or 9-inch layers.

Yogurt Pound Cake with Apricot Yogurt Frosting

OATMEAL CAKE

Makes 8 to 10 servings

1½ cups water
1 cup uncooked quick oats
½ cup (1 stick) butter or margarine
2 cups C & H Dark Brown Sugar, packed
2 eggs

1½ cups all-purpose flour
1 teaspoon EACH baking powder *and* cinnamon
½ teaspoon EACH nutmeg *and* salt
Sugar Topping or Lazy Daisy Frosting (recipes follow)

Preheat oven to 350°F. Grease and flour 9-inch tube pan or 13x9-inch pan. Bring water to boil in large saucepan. Stir in oats. Remove from heat. Add butter, cover pan and let stand 15 minutes.

Combine sugar, eggs, flour, baking powder, cinnamon, nutmeg and salt. Add to oat mixture, mix well. Pour thin batter into pan. Bake 40 to 45 minutes (tube pan) or 25 to 30 minutes (shallow pan). Cool tube cake in pan 10 minutes, then turn out onto serving plate. While hot, add Sugar Topping or Lazy Daisy Frosting.

Variation—Oatmeal Cupcakes: Pour batter into 18 paper-lined muffin cups. Bake 20 minutes. Prick hot cupcakes and spoon on hot topping. Serve warm or cold.

Sugar Topping

¼ cup C & H Dark Brown Sugar, packed
¼ cup (½ stick) butter or margarine

1 tablespoon water
1 teaspoon vanilla

Combine all ingredients in small saucepan. Heat until butter melts. Prick hot cake with skewer or fork. Pour hot topping over cake. Serve warm or cold.

Lazy Daisy Frosting

¼ cup (½ stick) butter or
    margarine
¼ cup evaporated milk

½ cup C & H Golden
    Brown Sugar, packed
1 cup flaked coconut
½ cup chopped walnuts

Heat butter and milk in small saucepan until butter melts. Stir in remaining ingredients. Spread evenly over hot cake. Place under broiler until bubbly. Serve warm or cold.

DOUBLE ORANGE CUPCAKES

Makes about 2 dozen

1¼ cups C & H Granulated
    Sugar
¾ cup (1½ sticks) butter or
    margarine, softened
3 eggs, separated
3 cups all-purpose flour
4 teaspoons baking
    powder

½ teaspoon salt
1 cup orange juice
    Pinch EACH salt *and*
    cream of tartar
1 teaspoon grated orange
    rind
    Orange Icing (recipe
    follows)

Preheat oven to 350°F. Cream sugar and butter. Beat in egg yolks. Combine flour, baking powder and ½ teaspoon salt. Add to batter alternately with orange juice beginning and ending with dry ingredients. Beat well after each addition. Beat egg whites with pinch of salt and cream of tartar until stiff peaks form. Fold into batter along with orange rind. Fill 24 paper-lined muffin cups half full. Bake 25 minutes. Frost with Orange Icing.

Orange Icing

2 cups C & H Powdered
    Sugar
3 tablespoons orange
    juice

1 teaspoon grated orange
    rind

Combine all ingredients and beat until smooth. Spoon icing over cupcakes. Let stand until firm.

CARROT LAYER CAKE

Makes 8 to 10 servings

2 cups C & H Dark Brown
   Sugar, packed
4 eggs
2 cups all-purpose flour
2 teaspoons EACH baking
   soda *and* cinnamon
¾ teaspoon salt
1½ cups vegetable oil
2 cups coarsely grated
   carrots
1 cup coarsely chopped
   walnuts
Orange Buttercream
   Frosting (recipe
   follows)

Preheat oven to 350°F. Grease and flour two 9-inch cake pans. Gradually beat sugar into eggs. Combine flour, soda, cinnamon and salt; add to egg mixture alternately with oil, beginning and ending with flour. Fold in carrots and walnuts. Pour batter into pans, dividing evenly. Bake 35 to 40 minutes. Cool 10 minutes in pans, then turn out onto rack to finish cooling. Frost with Orange Buttercream Frosting.

Orange Buttercream Frosting

4 cups C & H Powdered
   Sugar
½ cup (1 stick) butter or
   margarine, softened
Pinch of salt
¼ cup orange juice
1 teaspoon grated orange
   rind

Combine all ingredients in bowl and beat about 3 minutes, until smooth and creamy. Frosts tops and sides of two 8-inch or 9-inch layers.

Carrot Layer Cake with Orange Buttercream Frosting

PINEAPPLE UPSIDE-DOWN CAKE

Makes 6 to 8 servings

3 tablespoons butter or
    margarine
½ cup C & H Brown
    Sugar, packed
4 to 6 slices canned
    pineapple (reserve ½
    cup syrup)
    Maraschino cherries
    Walnut halves

¾ cup C & H Brown
    Sugar, packed
¼ cup (½ stick) butter or
    margarine, softened
1 egg
1 teaspoon vanilla
1¼ cups all-purpose flour
1½ teaspoons baking
    powder
¼ teaspoon salt

Preheat oven to 350°F. Melt 3 tablespoons butter in 8-inch square pan or deep 9-inch round pan. Sprinkle with ½ cup brown sugar. Arrange pineapple slices, cherries and walnuts over sugar; set aside.

Cream ¾ cup brown sugar and ¼ cup butter until fluffy. Beat in egg and vanilla. Combine flour, baking powder and salt. Add to creamed mixture alternately with pineapple syrup, beating until smooth after each addition. Spread batter over pineapple. Bake 40 to 45 minutes or until cake tester inserted in center comes out clean. Let rest 5 minutes, then turn cake upside down on serving plate. Serve warm.

Variation — Papaya Upside-Down Cake: Marinate 2 cups sliced papaya in 2 tablespoons lemon juice 15 minutes. Substitute for pineapple slices. Sprinkle with ¼ cup toasted sliced almonds. Omit walnuts and cherries. Substitute ½ cup milk for pineapple syrup.

CARROT PINEAPPLE CAKE

Makes 10 to 12 servings

2 cups C & H Granulated Sugar
3 eggs
1½ cups vegetable oil
1 teaspoon vanilla
2 cups finely shredded carrots
1 can (8½ ounces) crushed pineapple, undrained

3¼ cups cake flour (or 2¾ cups all-purpose flour less 2½ tablespoons)
2 teaspoons EACH baking powder *and* cinnamon
1 teaspoon EACH baking soda *and* nutmeg
½ teaspoon salt
Orange Frosting (recipe follows) or C & H Powdered Sugar

Preheat oven to 350°F. Grease and flour 10-inch tube pan. In large bowl, combine granulated sugar, eggs, oil and vanilla; beat well. Stir in carrots and pineapple. Combine flour, baking powder, cinnamon, soda, nutmeg and salt. Blend into batter. Pour into pan. Bake 60 to 70 minutes or until cake tester inserted in center comes out clean. Cool in pan 10 minutes. With long spatula, loosen edges and turn out onto rack to finish cooling. Frost with Orange Frosting or sprinkle with powdered sugar.

Orange Frosting

2 cups C & H Powdered Sugar
2 tablespoons butter or margarine, softened
1 egg, separated
¼ teaspoon salt

1 to 2 tablespoons grated orange rind
½ teaspoon grated lemon rind
Orange juice
Pinch EACH salt *and* cream of tartar

Cream sugar, butter, egg yolk and salt until fluffy. Stir in orange and lemon rinds; add enough orange juice to make a spreading consistency. Beat egg white with salt and cream of tartar until stiff; fold into mixture.

75

SOUR CREAM SPICE CAKE

Makes 8 servings

1¼ cups C & H Golden Brown Sugar, packed
½ cup (1 stick) butter or margarine, softened
3 eggs
1¾ cups all-purpose flour
2 teaspoons baking powder
1 teaspoon cinnamon
½ teaspoon EACH allspice, nutmeg *and* baking soda
¼ teaspoon salt
¾ cup sour cream
½ cup chopped walnuts
Sour Cream Frosting (recipe follows)
Chocolate Glaze (recipe follows)
½ cup walnut halves

Preheat oven to 350°F. Grease and flour two 8-inch cake pans. Cream sugar and butter. Add eggs, 1 at a time, beating well after each addition. Combine flour, baking powder, cinnamon, allspice, nutmeg, soda and salt. Add to creamed mixture alternately with sour cream, beginning and ending with dry ingredients. Stir in chopped walnuts. Spoon into pans. Bake 30 to 35 minutes or until cake tester inserted in center comes out clean. Cool in pans 10 minutes on rack, then turn out onto racks to finish cooling. Frost with Sour Cream Frosting. Pour Chocolate Glaze over top and garnish with walnut halves.

Sour Cream Frosting

4 cups C & H Powdered Sugar
½ cup (1 stick) butter or margarine, softened
3 tablespoons sour cream
1 teaspoon vanilla
Pinch of salt

Combine all ingredients and beat 5 minutes until smooth and creamy. Makes 2¼ cups; enough to frost two 8-inch layers.

Chocolate Glaze

2 ounces (2 squares)
   unsweetened
   chocolate

2 teaspoons butter

Melt chocolate and butter over low heat; stir until well blended.

JEAN'S GINGERBREAD

Makes 12 servings

1 cup C & H Golden
   Brown Sugar, packed
½ cup shortening
2 eggs
2 cups all-purpose flour
1 teaspoon EACH baking
   soda, salt, cinnamon
   and ground ginger

¼ teaspoon ground cloves
½ cup molasses
½ cup boiling water
   C & H Powdered Sugar

Preheat oven to 350°F. Grease and flour 13x9-inch pan. In large bowl, combine brown sugar and shortening; beat well. Add eggs, 1 at a time, beating well after each addition. Combine flour, soda, salt, cinnamon, ginger and cloves. Blend molasses and water. Add flour and molasses mixtures alternately to batter, beginning and ending with dry ingredients. Pour into pan. Bake 40 minutes. Cool in pan. Cut into squares. Sprinkle with powdered sugar. Serve warm or cold.

AUNT NELLIE'S RAISIN CAKE

Makes 12 servings

1 cup raisins
2 cups water
1½ cups C & H Dark Brown
   Sugar, packed
½ cup shortening
2 eggs
3 cups all-purpose flour
2 teaspoons cinnamon

1 teaspoon EACH salt *and*
   nutmeg
½ teaspoon ground cloves
1 teaspoon baking soda
1 cup chopped walnuts
   Creamy Lemon Frosting
   (recipe follows) or
   C & H Powdered
   Sugar

Preheat oven to 350°F. Grease 13x9-inch baking pan. Combine raisins and water in saucepan. Cover and simmer 10 minutes. Drain, reserving 1 cup simmering liquid (add water, if necessary, to fill cup). Cream sugar and shortening. Beat in eggs. Combine flour, cinnamon, salt, nutmeg and cloves. Stir soda into reserved raisin liquid. Add dry ingredients and raisin liquid alternately to creamed mixture, mixing well after each addition. Stir in drained raisins and walnuts. Pour into pan. Bake 35 to 40 minutes. Cool in pan. Frost with Creamy Lemon Frosting or sprinkle with powdered sugar.

Creamy Lemon Frosting

2 cups C & H Powdered
   Sugar
¼ cup (½ stick) butter or
   margarine, softened

½ teaspoon grated lemon
   rind
1½ tablespoons lemon juice

Cream sugar and butter. Stir in lemon rind and juice; beat until creamy and smooth. Add more lemon juice, if necessary, to make a good spreading consistency.

Note: Double this recipe to frost a 2-layer cake.

BANANA CAKE

Makes 12 servings

1¼ cups C & H Granulated Sugar
½ cup (1 stick) butter or margarine
½ teaspoon nutmeg
2 eggs
1 cup mashed ripe bananas (2 to 3 medium)
1 teaspoon vanilla

2½ cups all-purpose flour
1¼ teaspoons baking powder
1 teaspoon EACH baking soda *and* salt
½ cup buttermilk
½ cup chopped nuts
Cream Cheese Frosting (recipe follows)

Preheat oven to 350°F. Grease 13x9-inch pan. Cream sugar, butter and nutmeg until fluffy. Add eggs, 1 at a time, beating well after each addition. Stir in bananas and vanilla. Combine flour, baking powder, soda and salt. Beat into creamed mixture alternately with buttermilk. Stir in nuts. Spread batter in pan. Bake 30 to 35 minutes or until cake tester inserted in center comes out clean. Cool on rack. Frost with Cream Cheese Frosting.

Cream Cheese Frosting

4 cups C & H Powdered Sugar
3 tablespoons milk
1 package (3 ounces) cream cheese, softened

¼ cup (½ stick) butter or margarine, softened
¼ cup chopped walnuts
¼ cup chopped raisins

Combine sugar, milk, cream cheese and butter; beat until smooth. Stir in walnuts and raisins.

BLUEBERRY SHORTCAKE

Makes 8 servings

Blueberry Filling (recipe
   follows)
2 tablespoons C & H
   Granulated Sugar
2 cups all-purpose flour
2½ teaspoons baking
   powder
¼ teaspoon salt

6 tablespoons (¾ stick)
   cold butter, coarsely
   chopped
⅔ cup light cream or
   milk
Softened butter or
   margarine
1 cup whipping cream,
   whipped

Prepare Blueberry Filling and set aside. Preheat oven to 450°F. Grease large cookie sheet. Mix sugar, flour, baking powder and salt. Cut in butter with pastry blender or fingertips until mixture resembles coarse meal. Make a well in center, pour in light cream, then stir with a fork just until dough holds together. Turn out onto lightly floured board. Knead for 1 minute. Pat into eight ½-inch-thick circles or roll into rectangle and cut with biscuit cutter. Arrange on cookie sheet. Bake 10 to 15 minutes, until brown. Cut in half horizontally and spread insides with butter. Fill bottom halves with Blueberry Filling and whipped cream. Cap with top halves.

Blueberry Filling

¾ cup C & H Granulated
   Sugar

2 tablespoons lemon juice
1 quart blueberries

In heavy saucepan, combine sugar, lemon juice and half the berries. Cook over very low heat until sugar melts; raise heat and cook 10 to 15 minutes until mixture thickens. Cool slightly, then stir in remaining berries.

APPLE CRISP

Makes 6 servings

1 cup C & H Golden
   Brown Sugar, packed
¼ cup (½ stick) butter or
   margarine, softened
½ cup all-purpose flour
½ teaspoon EACH
   cinnamon *and*
   nutmeg

¼ teaspoon salt
5 cups sliced peeled
   apples (5 to 6
   medium)
Sweetened whipped
   cream or ice cream

Preheat oven to 350°F. Grease 8- or 9-inch square pan. Mix sugar, butter, flour, cinnamon, nutmeg and salt with pastry blender or fingertips until mixture resembles coarse meal. Spread apples over bottom of pan. Sprinkle crumbly mixture over apples. Pat lightly with fingers. Bake 50 to 60 minutes, or until apples are tender. Serve warm with whipped cream or ice cream.

VELVET POUND CAKE

Makes 8 servings

2¼ cups C & H Powdered
   Sugar
¾ cup (1½ sticks) butter or
   margarine, softened
½ teaspoon nutmeg or
   ¼ teaspoon mace

½ teaspoon vanilla
½ teaspoon grated lemon
   rind or lemon extract
3 eggs
1½ cups all-purpose flour
   C & H Powdered Sugar

Preheat oven to 325°F. Grease 9x5x3-inch loaf pan. Cream 2¼ cups sugar, the butter, nutmeg, vanilla and lemon rind. Beat in 1 egg, then ¼ cup flour; repeat until all eggs are used. Add remaining flour and beat until smooth. Spread thick batter in loaf pan. Cut through batter several times with knife to break large air bubbles. Bake 60 to 70 minutes or until cake tester inserted in center comes out clean. (Top will have a rough crack.) Remove from pan immediately and cool right side up on rack. Sprinkle with sugar.

PECAN PIE

Makes 8 servings

1 unbaked 9-inch Butter
   Pie Crust (recipe
   follows)
1 cup C & H Golden
   Brown Sugar, packed
3 eggs
¾ cup corn syrup

¼ cup (½ stick) butter or
   margarine, melted
1 teaspoon vanilla
¼ teaspoon salt
1 cup coarsely chopped
   pecans
Pecan halves

Prepare pie crust. Preheat oven to 375°F. Combine sugar and eggs; beat well. Beat in corn syrup, butter, vanilla and salt. Stir in chopped pecans. Pour filling into pie crust. Garnish with pecan halves. Bake 40 to 45 minutes or until center of filling is firm when pan is gently shaken. Cool to room temperature.

BUTTER PIE CRUST

Makes single 8- or 9-inch crust

¼ cup C & H Powdered
   Sugar
1 cup all-purpose flour
⅛ teaspoon salt

6 tablespoons (¾ stick)
   cold butter or
   margarine, cut in
   pieces
3 tablespoons ice water
2 to 3 cups dried beans
   (for weight)

Combine sugar, flour and salt in bowl. Add butter and mix with pastry blender or fingertips until mixture resembles coarse meal. Add water. Gather pastry into a ball and pat into flat round. Wrap in plastic wrap and chill 1 hour.

On a lightly floured surface, roll pastry into a circle ⅛ inch thick and fit into a lightly greased 9-inch pie pan. Trim edge evenly, then flute or crimp decoratively. Place in freezer at least 15 minutes while preheating oven to 425°F.

Line pie crust with greased waxed paper or parchment and fill with dried beans (to weigh down crust). Bake 15 minutes, until edges brown and crust is firm enough to support itself. Remove paper and beans. Prick bottom of crust with a fork. For a partially baked crust, bake 5 minutes longer, until lightly browned. For a fully baked crust, bake 10 minutes longer, until completely browned.

Note: Rolled or unrolled pastry can be stored 1 week in the refrigerator before it is baked. For freshest pastry, bake crust the day it is to be served.

BANANA-BUTTERSCOTCH PIE

Makes 8 servings

1 baked 9-inch Butter Pie
   Crust (see preceding
   recipe)
¾ cup C & H Golden
   Brown Sugar, packed
⅓ cup flour
¼ teaspoon salt
2 cups milk

2 eggs
1 tablespoon butter or
   margarine
1 teaspoon vanilla
3 large ripe bananas
   Sweetened whipped
   cream

Prepare pie crust and let cool. In heavy saucepan, combine sugar, flour and salt. Stir in half of the milk and mix until smooth. Bring to boil over medium heat, stirring constantly. Boil 2 minutes longer, until thick and smooth; remove from heat. With fork, beat eggs with remaining 1 cup milk; gradually stir into hot mixture. Return to heat and boil 2 minutes, stirring. Blend in butter and vanilla. Place a sheet of plastic wrap directly on custard so crust doesn't form; cool.

Slice bananas and arrange in pie crust. Pour cooled custard over bananas. Chill. Before serving, top with whipped cream.

Variation — Banana Cream Pie: Substitute C & H Granulated Sugar for C & H Golden Brown Sugar.

SOUR CREAM APPLE PIE

Makes 8 servings

1 unbaked 9-inch pie crust
   (see index)
5 large tart apples
1 tablespoon lemon juice
$3/4$ cup C & H Granulated
   Sugar
$1/3$ cup all-purpose flour

1 teaspoon cinnamon
$1/4$ teaspoon EACH nutmeg
   and salt
$1/4$ cup ($1/2$ stick) butter or
   margarine, softened
$1/2$ cup sour cream

Prepare pie crust. Preheat oven to 350°F. Peel apples and cut into thick slices. Arrange slices in overlapping rows in pastry-lined pie pan; sprinkle with lemon juice. Blend sugar, flour, cinnamon, nutmeg and salt. Cut in butter with pastry blender or fingertips until mixture resembles coarse meal; spoon over apples. Spread sour cream over top. Bake 45 to 50 minutes, until apples are tender.

SOUR CREAM RAISIN PIE

Makes 6 to 8 servings

1 baked 9-inch pie crust
   (see index)
1 cup C & H Granulated
   Sugar
2 tablespoons all-purpose
   flour
$1/2$ teaspoon EACH
   cinnamon *and*
   nutmeg

$1/4$ teaspoon salt
$1/2$ pint (1 cup) sour cream
2 eggs, beaten
$3/4$ cup seedless raisins
   Sweetened whipped
   cream

Prepare pie crust. Combine sugar, flour, cinnamon, nutmeg and salt in top of double boiler. Stir in sour cream. Place over boiling water. Cook about 5 minutes, stirring constantly, until slightly thickened. Gradually beat hot mixture into eggs. Add raisins. Pour mixture into double boiler and cook 5 minutes, stirring occasionally. Cool. Spoon into baked pie crust. Chill. Before serving, top with whipped cream.

Sour Cream Apple Pie

ALL-AMERICAN APPLE PIE

Makes 8 servings

1 cup C & H Granulated
  Sugar
6 to 7 medium apples,
  peeled, cored and
  sliced 1/8 inch thick
1 tablespoon lemon juice
1/4 teaspoon cinnamon
1/8 teaspoon nutmeg
1 unbaked 9-inch No-Fail
  Pie Crust (recipe
  follows)

1 tablespoon butter or
  margarine
1 egg white (or 1
  tablespoon cream or
  milk)
1 tablespoon C & H
  Granulated Sugar
Vanilla ice cream or
  cheddar cheese slices
  (optional)

Combine 1 cup sugar, the apples, lemon juice, cinnamon and nutmeg in bowl. Marinate 1 hour, stirring occasionally.

Preheat oven to 450°F. Prepare pastry and line pie pan with half. Drain apples, reserving juice, and arrange in pie pan. Dot with butter and add top crust. Brush top crust with egg white and sprinkle with 1 tablespoon sugar. Cut 4 slits in top crust. Bake pie 15 minutes. Reduce heat to 375°F and bake 30 minutes longer or until apples are tender when pierced with knife through slit.

Meanwhile, in small heavy saucepan, cook reserved apple juice over low heat until sugar dissolves. Raise heat and boil until reduced by about half. Remove from heat before juice caramelizes. Pour juice through slits in crust, tilting pie pan to distribute evenly. If filling appears dry, use all the juice; if not, adjust amount accordingly so pie doesn't become soggy. Serve warm or cold with ice cream or cheese, if desired.

NO-FAIL PIE CRUST

Makes double 9- or 10-inch crust

1 tablespoon C & H Granulated Sugar	¹⁄₂ cup water
4 cups all-purpose flour	1 egg
2 teaspoons salt	1 tablespoon white vinegar
1³⁄₄ cups shortening	

Combine sugar, flour and salt in bowl. Add shortening and mix with fork or pastry blender until crumbly. Beat water, egg and vinegar together. Add to flour mixture; mix until all ingredients are moistened. Form into flat circle. Chill at least 15 minutes before forming.

On lightly floured board or pastry cloth, roll half of dough into a circle with quick light strokes, working outward from center. Lift up dough occasionally and dust with just enough flour to keep from sticking. When circle is 1¹⁄₂ inches larger than inverted pie pan, gently ease it into greased pan. Trim edge, add desired filling; moisten rim of bottom pastry with water. Roll top crust and place over filling; trim and seal 2 edges together; crimp decoratively. Cut slits in top crust for steam to escape. Bake according to recipe directions.

Single Crusts: (Makes 2. Freeze 1 for later use.) Roll out pastry, line pie pans and trim edges, leaving ¹⁄₂-inch overhang. Turn edges under; crimp. Prick well with fork. To prebake, bake in preheated 475°F oven 8 to 10 minutes until golden brown.

GRANDMA COOPER'S PEACH PIE

Long, slow simmering creates the unique flavor of "candied" peaches

Makes 8 servings

1 cup C & H Granulated Sugar	2 tablespoons quick-cooking tapioca
½ cup water	¼ teaspoon cinnamon
5 cups peeled, thickly sliced peaches	2 tablespoons butter or margarine
1 unbaked 9-inch double pie crust (see index)	Sweetened whipped cream or sliced cheese

In large, heavy saucepan, cook sugar and water over low heat until sugar dissolves. Bring to boil, add peaches, cover pan and poach over gentle heat 45 minutes. (Liquid should barely move.)

While peaches are simmering, prepare pastry and line pie pan with half, trimming with scissors to leave a ½-inch border above the edge. With slotted spoon, transfer peaches to unbaked pie crust, sprinkling a little tapioca and cinnamon over each layer. Boil down poaching syrup to ½ cup; pour over peaches and dot with butter.

Preheat oven to 425°F. Using remaining pastry, cut ½-inch-wide strips and weave a lattice top. Moisten edge of crust and press strips to edge. Fold border of bottom crust up over ends of strips; crimp edge. Bake 30 minutes or until crust is browned. Cool to lukewarm on rack. Serve slightly warm with whipped cream or cheese.

LEMON BLOSSOM PIE

Makes 6 to 8 servings

1 baked 8-inch pie crust (see index)
1 cup C & H Granulated Sugar
1/4 cup cornstarch
1/4 teaspoon salt
1 1/2 cups boiling water
3 eggs, separated
2 teaspoons grated lemon rind
1/3 cup lemon juice (2 to 3 lemons)
2 tablespoons butter or margarine
Pinch EACH salt *and* cream of tartar
1/2 cup C & H Granulated or Superfine Sugar

Prepare pie crust. Combine 1 cup sugar, the cornstarch and 1/4 teaspoon salt in saucepan. Gradually stir in boiling water and cook, stirring constantly 2 to 3 minutes until mixture is clear and thickened. Remove from heat. Combine egg yolks, lemon rind and lemon juice; stir carefully into hot mixture. Cook, stirring, 3 minutes longer. Remove from heat and add butter. Cool 5 minutes. Pour into baked pie crust.

Preheat oven to 350°F. Beat egg whites with pinch salt and cream of tartar until soft peaks form. Add 1/2 cup sugar, 1 tablespoon at a time; continue to beat until stiff and glossy. Swirl meringue over pie, sealing to crust. Bake 12 to 14 minutes, until golden brown.

Variation — Lime Blossom Pie: Substitute lime rind and juice for lemon.

Hint: A meringue for a shell is beaten enough when you can no longer feel the grains of sugar when you rub a bit of the meringue between thumb and forefinger.

FLUFFY COCONUT CREAM PIE

Makes 8 servings

1 **baked 9-inch pie crust (see index)**	2 **eggs, separated**
²/₃ **cup C & H Granulated Sugar**	1 **tablespoon butter**
2¹/₂ **tablespoons cornstarch**	1¹/₂ **teaspoons vanilla**
1 **tablespoon flour**	³/₄ **cup flaked coconut**
¹/₂ **teaspoon salt**	**Pinch EACH salt** *and* **cream of tartar**
3 **cups milk**	**Sweetened whipped cream**

Prepare pie crust. In heavy saucepan, combine half the sugar, the cornstarch, flour and ¹/₂ teaspoon salt. Stir in 2 cups of the milk and mix until smooth. Bring to boil over medium heat, stirring constantly. Boil gently 2 minutes longer until thick and smooth. Remove from heat. With fork, beat egg yolks with remaining 1 cup milk; gradually stir into hot mixture. Return to heat and boil 2 minutes, stirring. Mix in butter, vanilla and coconut. Place a sheet of plastic wrap directly on custard so crust doesn't form; cool.

Beat egg whites with pinch salt and cream of tartar until soft peaks form. Add remaining ¹/₃ cup sugar, 1 tablespoon at a time; continue to beat until stiff peaks form. Fold meringue into custard. Pour into pie crust; chill. Before serving, top with whipped cream.

4 FROZEN FINALES

These make-ahead marvels are easy but elegant

Frozen desserts are the answer to every hostess's prayer. Not only are they the perfect encore for a midsummer meal; they offer the indisputable advantage of being ready whenever you are. Whether it's for unexpected guests, a party so elaborate that some things must be made ahead or the ordinary pressures of a business and social lifestyle, frozen desserts are the elegant answer.

While ice creams made in the freezer never have the same smooth creaminess as those made in a freezing machine with a churn, frozen parfaits and mousses are gossamer in texture and slip down with silken ease.

To most Americans, the word mousse evokes thoughts of an airy chocolate custard they've enjoyed in fine restaurants and a parfait has got to be a multi-colored layering of ice creams and syrup in a tall crystal glass. The culinary profession has differing definitions, but the only point on which experts agree is that both parfaits and dessert mousses are made with sweetened whipped cream and do not require beating during the freezing process. We prefer to acknowledge the public's conceptions and have further defined mousse as a custard-like mixture which is aerated with egg whites and formed in a mold. Our parfaits have a texture similar to ice cream and are scooped into glasses, whether layered or not.

Any mousse or parfait, if layered into a fancy mold, could become a bombe. Mousses can also be transformed into spectacular frozen soufflés by selecting a straight-sided dish with 2 to 2½ cups less volume than the mold specified and adding a soufflé collar.

To make a soufflé collar, fold an 8-inch wide band of aluminum foil in half lengthwise, grease it well and wrap it around the soufflé dish so that it extends 3 inches above the rim. Secure with a string or clip the ends together with a straight pin or paper clip. Gently remove collar before serving. Macaroon crumbs, ground nuts or grated chocolate may be pressed into the side of the soufflé for decoration.

Fruit ices such as sherbets (made with sweetened juice and milk, egg white or gelatin) and granitas (made with sweetened juice and water alone) need to be beaten during the freezing process. Sherbets have a smoother texture, while granitas are enjoyed for the icy graininess of their texture.

Orange and lemon shells make attractive containers for serving frozen ices. Cut the required number of oranges or lemons in half, using a sawtooth cut to make fluted edges. Squeeze out the juice and scrape out the pulp. Freeze the shells and pack with sherbet or granita just before serving. Garnish each serving with a sprig of mint for a touch of color.

You can create the illusion of a vast repertoire of frozen desserts by merely varying the molded shape or container, by combining two or more in layers or by switching sauces and toppings.

Back to front: Coffee Parfait (page 96) in Meringue Shell (page 129) with Chocolate Sauce (page 97), Apricot Parfait in Crisp Cookie Cups (page 94), Rhubarb Mousse (page 95)

APRICOT PARFAIT

Photograph on page 93

Makes 8 servings

1 pound fresh apricots or 10 canned apricots, drained	1 tablespoon brandy
1½ cups C & H Superfine or Powdered Sugar	1 cup whipping cream
Juice of 1 lemon	8 Crisp Cookie Cups (recipe follows)
	Mint sprigs (optional)

Chop or sieve apricots to make 1¾ cups puree. Stir in sugar, lemon juice and brandy. Whip cream until stiff; fold into puree. Freeze overnight. To serve, spoon parfait into Crisp Cookie Cups and garnish with mint sprigs.

Crisp Cookie Cups

Makes 8 cookie cups

½ cup C & H Granulated Sugar	Grated rind of 1 lemon
¼ cup (½ stick) butter, softened	2 egg whites
	⅓ cup all-purpose flour

Preheat oven to 425°F. Grease and flour 2 large cookie sheets. Using a saucer, trace 4 circles about 5½ inches in diameter on each cookie sheet. Lightly grease 8 coffee cups or bowls about 2 inches in diameter. Beat sugar, butter and lemon rind together until fluffy. Mix in egg whites just until blended. Fold flour into batter. Place 1½ tablespoons batter in center of each circle on cookie sheet. With back of spoon, spread batter in thin even layer over circles. Bake about 5 minutes or until cookies brown around edges. Wait 1 minute, then remove cookies with a spatula and press into prepared coffee cups. When firm, transfer to rack. If cookies become too stiff to form, return to oven for several seconds. If cookies are not to be served the day they are made, freeze until needed.

Variation: Create ''saucers'' by doubling the recipe and allowing half the circles to firm on cookie sheet after baking.

RHUBARB MOUSSE

Photograph on page 93

Makes 8 to 10 servings

1½ cups C & H Granulated
    Sugar
½ cup water
6 egg whites
1 pinch EACH salt *and*
    cream of tartar
2 cups whipping cream
¼ teaspoon cinnamon

2 cups cooked rhubarb
    puree
2 pints strawberries
½ cup C & H Powdered
    Sugar
2 tablespoons kirsch, rum
    or brandy

Combine granulated sugar and water in small heavy saucepan. Cook over low heat until sugar dissolves, swirling pan occasionally. Raise heat and cook without stirring until syrup reaches 236°F on candy thermometer (soft ball stage). Meanwhile, beat egg whites with salt and cream of tartar until stiff peaks form. Gradually add syrup and continue beating about 10 minutes, until mixture is cool and thick. Whip cream until stiff and gently fold into beaten egg-white mixture. Cover and freeze 2 hours.

Stir cinnamon into rhubarb puree and then mix puree into frozen cream. Pour into 8-cup ring mold or 8 individual molds. Freeze at least 2 more hours until firm. Marinate strawberries with powdered sugar and kirsch. To serve, unmold rhubarb mousse onto chilled serving plate(s). Fill center(s) with marinated strawberries.

COFFEE PARFAIT

Photograph on page 93

Makes 4 to 6 servings

½ cup C & H Powdered
    Sugar
6 egg yolks
¾ cup strong liquid coffee
1 cup whipping cream

Individual Meringue
    Shells (see index)
Chocolate Sauce (see
    next page)

Beat sugar and egg yolks together until thick and lemon-colored. Beat in liquid coffee. Transfer to heavy saucepan or top of double boiler and stir over low heat 2 minutes or until mixture is thick enough so bottom of pan can be seen between strokes. Remove from heat and beat until cool. Whip cream until stiff and gently fold into coffee mixture. Cover and freeze at least 4 hours. To serve, spoon into Meringue Shells, top with Chocolate Sauce.

Note: Coffee Parfait may also be served in individual dessert glasses, topped with sweetened whipped cream and sprinkled with freshly ground coffee powder.

BLACKBERRY MOUSSE

Makes 4 to 6 servings

⅔ cup C & H Granulated
    Sugar
3 eggs, separated
½ pint blackberries,
    pureed and sieved to
    eliminate seeds
2 tablespoons cassis,
    brandy or kirsch
    (optional)

1 tablespoon lemon juice
    Pinch EACH salt *and*
    cream of tartar
1 cup whipping cream
    Additional blackberries
    (optional)

Combine sugar, egg yolks and blackberry puree in mixing bowl. Place in pan containing water and beat over medium heat until sugar is dissolved and mixture is thick and hot to the touch. Remove from heat and continue beating until cool. Stir in cassis and lemon juice. In separate bowl, beat egg whites with salt and cream of tartar until stiff. Stir about ¼ of egg whites into blackberry mixture to aerate, then fold in the rest. Beat cream until softly whipped and fold into mixture. Turn into 1-quart mold and freeze 6 hours or until firm. Unmold and transfer to refrigerator 30 minutes before serving. Garnish with additional fresh berries, if desired.

PISTACHIO PARFAIT

Makes 4 servings

¾ cup C & H Superfine or Granulated Sugar	⅓ cup pistachios, husked and ground
4 egg yolks	1 cup whipping cream (optional)
½ cup milk	
2 teaspoons vanilla	Chocolate Sauce (recipe follows)

Combine sugar, egg yolks and milk in mixing bowl. Place in pan containing water and beat over medium heat until sugar is dissolved and mixture is thick, lemon-colored and hot to the touch. Remove from heat and continue beating until cool. Stir in vanilla and pistachios, reserving 1½ tablespoons ground nuts for garnish. Beat cream until softly whipped. Stir about ¼ of cream into pistachio mixture to aerate, then fold in the rest. Freeze 4 to 6 hours, until firm. Transfer to refrigerator 30 minutes before serving. Spoon parfait into goblets, top with Chocolate Sauce and sprinkle with reserved nuts.

Chocolate Sauce

¼ cup C & H Powdered Sugar	2 tablespoons butter
3 ounces unsweetened chocolate	

Combine sugar and chocolate in top of double boiler. Melt over simmering water. Whisk in butter and stir until smooth.

LEMON PARFAIT

Serve this dessert in a glass that shows off to advantage its vivid color contrasts

Makes 4 to 6 servings

1 cup C & H Powdered Sugar	2 teaspoons grated lemon rind
6 egg yolks	1 cup whipping cream
½ cup lemon juice	Blueberry Sauce (recipe follows)

Beat sugar and egg yolks together until thick and lemon-colored. Beat in lemon juice. Transfer to heavy saucepan or top of double boiler and stir over low heat 2 minutes or until mixture is thick enough to see bottom of pan between strokes. Remove from heat and beat until cool. Stir in lemon rind. Whip cream until stiff and gently fold into yolk mixture. Cover and freeze at least 4 hours. To serve, spoon into dessert glasses or bowls and top with a spoonful of chilled Blueberry Sauce. Pass remaining sauce in a sauceboat.

Blueberry Sauce

½ cup C & H Granulated Sugar	1 teaspoon cornstarch dissolved in ¼ cup cold water
1 pint blueberries Juice of 1 lemon	

Place sugar, blueberries and lemon juice in saucepan and stir over medium heat until sugar dissolves. Add cornstarch and cook until thickened. Cool, then chill.

Note: Try Blueberry Sauce over pancakes or waffles for a special treat.

Lemon Parfait with Blueberry Sauce

RASPBERRY PARFAIT

Makes 4 to 6 servings

¾ cup C & H Granulated Sugar
¼ cup water
3 egg whites
Pinch EACH salt *and* cream of tartar
½ pint raspberries, pureed and sieved to remove seeds
1 cup whipping cream

2 tablespoons kirsch, rum or Grand Marnier (optional)
1 additional pint raspberries
¼ cup C & H Powdered Sugar
2 additional tablespoons liqueur

Combine granulated sugar and water in small heavy saucepan. Cook over low heat until sugar dissolves, swirling pan occasionally. Increase heat and cook until sugar syrup reaches 236°F on candy thermometer (soft ball stage). Meanwhile, beat egg whites with salt and cream of tartar until stiff peaks form. Gradually beat in sugar syrup and continue beating until mixture is thick and cool. Stir in raspberry puree. Beat cream and kirsch together until softly whipped. Stir about ¼ of whipped cream into raspberry mixture to aerate, then fold in the rest. Freeze 4 to 6 hours until firm. Marinate additional raspberries with powdered sugar and kirsch. Transfer frozen raspberry parfait to refrigerator 30 minutes before serving. Spoon into goblets, layering with marinated raspberries.

Note: Raspberry parfait can also be frozen in a ring mold and served with marinated raspberries in the center.

ALMOND CARAMEL DELIGHT

Makes 10 to 12 servings

Almond Praline (recipe
follows)
4 eggs
½ cup C & H Granulated
Sugar

¼ cup water
1 tablespoon almond
liqueur or vanilla
1 cup whipping cream

Prepare Almond Praline. Beat eggs about 10 minutes or until thick, tripled in volume and lemon-colored. Meanwhile, combine sugar and water in large heavy saucepan. Cook over low heat until sugar dissolves, swirling pan occasionally. Raise heat and boil until sugar syrup reaches 236°F on candy thermometer (soft ball stage). Gradually beat sugar syrup into eggs. Return entire mixture to saucepan and stir over low heat until mixture is thick and warm and bottom of pan can be seen between strokes. Do not boil. Place over a bowl of ice water to cool, stirring occasionally. Stir in almond liqueur and chopped praline, reserving 2 tablespoons praline for garnish. Beat cream until softly whipped and fold into mixture. Pour into 1½-quart rectangular bread pan and freeze 6 hours or until firm. Unmold and transfer to refrigerator 30 minutes before serving. To serve, top with reserved praline and slice with serrated knife.

Almond Praline

⅔ cup C & H Granulated
Sugar
¼ cup water

½ cup sliced almonds,
plain or toasted

Grease cookie sheet. Combine sugar and water in small heavy saucepan. Cook over low heat until sugar dissolves, swirling pan occasionally. Raise heat and boil until sugar caramelizes, washing down any sugar crystals on sides of pan with brush dipped in cold water. Stir in almonds and pour out onto cookie sheet. When hard, chop finely.

LEMON GRANITA

Makes 6 to 8 servings

¼ cup C & H Superfine or
   Granulated Sugar
1½ cups water
1 teaspoon grated lemon
   rind (optional)

¼ cup freshly squeezed
   lemon juice
6 to 8 sprigs mint
   (optional)

Stir sugar, water, lemon rind and lemon juice together in bowl until sugar dissolves. Freeze 6 hours, until solid, beating every 2 hours to break up ice crystals. Before serving, beat in food processor or blender to smooth texture or scrape with a fork and mound in goblets or frozen lemon shells. Garnish with mint.

MELON SHERBET

Makes 4 to 6 servings

¾ cup C & H Granulated
   Sugar
1¼ cups water
1 medium cantaloupe

1 tablespoon lemon juice
1 egg white
4 sprigs mint (optional)

Combine sugar and water in small heavy saucepan. Cook over low heat until sugar dissolves, then cover pan and simmer 5 minutes. Cool. Halve cantaloupe, discard seeds and puree pulp. (You should have 3 cups.) Stir in lemon juice, egg white and cooled sugar syrup. Freeze in ice cream machine, following manufacturer's instructions, or turn into bowl and freeze about 6 hours, until solid, beating every 2 hours to break up ice crystals. To serve, scrape sherbet with a fork or paddle and mound in goblets. Garnish with mint.

Variation: For an attractive presentation, serve sherbet in frozen melon shells. Cut 2 cantaloupes in half with sawtooth edges to make 4 fluted halves. Use the pulp from 2 halves to make sherbet. Scoop pulp from second 2 halves to make melon balls. Refrigerate melon balls and freeze 4 fluted containers. At serving time, divide sherbet among containers and garnish with melon balls and mint.

CHOCOLATE ICE CREAM PIE

Makes 6 to 8 servings

1/4 cup C & H Granulated
   Sugar
1 1/2 cups blanched almonds,
   toasted and ground
1/3 cup butter
1 ounce semisweet
   chocolate
1 quart chocolate ice
   cream, slightly
   softened

Creamy Chocolate
   Sauce (recipe follows)
Sweetened whipped
   cream (optional)
1/2 cup sliced almonds,
   toasted

Combine sugar and ground almonds in bowl. Melt butter and chocolate together and stir into nut mixture. Pat mixture into lightly greased 9-inch pie pan. Chill 1 hour or until set. Spread chocolate ice cream in crust. Freeze until serving time. Top with Creamy Chocolate Sauce, sweetened whipped cream and sliced almonds.

Creamy Chocolate Sauce

1/3 cup C & H Powdered
   Sugar
2 ounces semisweet
   chocolate

1/3 cup whipping cream
1 tablespoon rum

Combine sugar, chocolate, cream and rum in top of double boiler. Heat, stirring occasionally, until smooth. Serve warm.

Hint: To fully savor desserts frozen for more than 6 hours, always refrigerate about 30 minutes before serving. Not only will texture and flavor be improved, but serving will be easier.

FLAMING BANANAS MARTINIQUE

An extravaganza of exotic tastes and textures

Makes 4 to 6 servings

Nougatine (recipe
  follows)
¼ cup C & H Dark Brown
  Sugar, packed
¼ cup (½ stick) butter
4 medium bananas, sliced
  diagonally ¼ inch
  thick

⅓ cup EACH coffee *and*
  almond liqueurs
⅓ cup rum
  Vanilla or coffee ice
  cream

Prepare nougatine. Melt sugar and butter in heavy skillet or chafing dish. Add bananas and cook 3 minutes or until just tender. Stir in coffee and almond liqueurs. Pour rum into a corner of pan. Ignite and shake pan until flames subside. Spoon over vanilla ice cream. Top with chopped nougatine.

Note: Bananas may be prepared up to 8 hours in advance. Leave at room temperature. Add rum and ignite when ready to serve.

Nougatine

¼ cup C & H Granulated
  Sugar
2 tablespoons water

⅓ cup coarsely chopped
  walnuts

Grease cookie sheet *with sides.* Combine sugar and water in small heavy saucepan. Cook over low heat until sugar dissolves, swirling pan occasionally. Raise heat and boil until sugar caramelizes, washing down any sugar crystals on sides of pan with brush dipped in cold water. Stir in walnuts and pour out onto greased cookie sheet. Chop coarsely when hard.

Flaming Bananas Martinique

MIXED BERRY JUBILEE

Makes 6 to 8 servings

½ cup C & H Granulated
   Sugar
½ cup water
1 tablespoon lemon juice
1½ pints mixed berries (i.e.
   blueberries, black-
   berries, strawberries
   or raspberries)

2 teaspoons cornstarch
   dissolved in 1
   tablespoon water
   (optional)
¼ cup brandy, kirsch or
   rum
   Vanilla ice cream

Combine sugar, water and lemon juice in small heavy saucepan or chafing dish. Cook over low heat until sugar dissolves, swirling pan occasionally. Cover pan and simmer 5 minutes over medium heat. Stir in berries and heat through. If desired, stir in cornstarch and simmer until thickened. Pour brandy into corner of saucepan. Ignite and shake pan until flames subside. Spoon over vanilla ice cream.

SURPRISE BAKED ALASKA

Makes 4 servings

2 egg whites
   Pinch EACH salt *and*
   cream of tartar
½ cup C & H Superfine or
   Granulated Sugar
1 cup halved strawberries

4 individual sponge cake
   shells
½ to 1 pint hard vanilla ice
   cream
4 whole strawberries

Preheat broiler. Beat egg whites with salt and cream of tartar until soft peaks form. Gradually beat in half the sugar, 1 tablespoon at a time, and continue beating until meringue is stiff and glossy. Mix remaining ¼ cup sugar with strawberry halves. Arrange sponge cakes on large wooden board or heatproof serving platter. Working quickly, fill cakes with a spoonful of ice cream, top with sugared berries, then cover completely with meringue, making decorative swirls. Place under broiler 1 to 2 minutes until lightly browned. Garnish with whole strawberries and serve immediately.

5 CROWNING GLORIES

*Masterpieces for company, holidays
and special occasions*

Special occasions call for special efforts and it's all worth it when your guests heap glowing compliments on your masterful creation. This chapter contains a variety of spectacular desserts to end an important meal, including that all-time favorite, a magnificent cake.

Ingredients for cakes should be at room temperature unless otherwise specified. This is particularly true for butter, eggs and liquids. Eggs separate more easily when cold, but allow them to come to room temperature before using.

Measure your ingredients accurately. Use graduated measuring cups and spoons for dry ingredients. For all-purpose flour and granulated sugar, dip the cup or spoon into the ingredient and level it off with a straight edge. Cake flour and powdered sugar are spooned lightly (never shaken or packed) into a cup before being leveled off. Nuts and shredded cheese are lightly packed; brown sugars and shortening, firmly packed. Butter may be measured before melting. Liquid should be measured in glass or transparent plastic measuring cup with the cup placed on a level surface and the measurement taken at eye level. When liquid is measured in spoonfuls, it's best to dip it from a small bowl or cup rather than pour it into the spoon.

Unless your oven is brand new, always preheat for about 10 minutes before baking. If you have any doubts about your oven's accuracy, test the temperature with an oven thermometer and adjust the oven controls accordingly.

Cake pans should be shiny, of the size specified in the recipe and prepared according to directions given. Grease pans lightly using shortening or sweet (unsalted) butter. If the pans are to be floured, shake the pans lightly to distribute the flour evenly, then invert them and tap out excess. To line and grease a pan, cut out a piece of waxed or parchment paper to fit the bottom of the pan, insert it and grease.

Cakes should be cooled before frosting. Cool layer cakes in their pans on a rack for 10 minutes before removing from pans to cool completely on the rack. To cool angel, sponge and chiffon cakes, suspend them on the neck of a bottle until completely cool—about 1½ hours.

To frost a layer cake, brush the layers free of any crumbs. Place the first layer upside down (flat surface on top) on a serving plate and insert strips of waxed paper under the edges to catch drippings. Cover the layer with frosting. Place the second layer topside down on the first and cover the sides and top of the cake lightly with frosting. Let the cake stand for about 15 minutes to harden the frosting and seal in any crumbs before lavishly coating the cake with the remaining frosting. Always frost the sides first; then the top.

Cakes freeze well. If frosted, freeze them uncovered for a few hours before wrapping for longer storage. Some cooks prefer cutting a cake into individual servings before freezing. Cakes made with whipped cream should be thawed in the refrigerator 3 to 4 hours. All others should be thawed in their wrappings at room temperature. Allow 30 minutes for cupcakes, 1 hour for unfrosted cakes and 2 hours for frosted cakes.

Cold Pumpkin Soufflé (page 110)

ALMOND COFFEE ROYALE

Makes 10 to 12 servings

1 cup C & H Granulated
   Sugar
4 eggs, separated
1½ cups cold milk
2 tablespoons instant
   coffee

1 package plain gelatin
   Pinch EACH salt *and*
   cream of tartar
1 cup whipping cream
1 cup sliced almonds,
   toasted

In top of double boiler, mix half the sugar, the egg yolks, 1¼ cups of the milk and the coffee. Soften gelatin in remaining ¼ cup milk. Add to coffee mixture and cook, stirring, over simmering water, about 15 minutes, until mixture thickens. Cool, then chill until mixture begins to set.

Beat egg whites with salt and cream of tartar until soft peaks form. Beat in remaining ½ cup sugar, 1 tablespoon at a time, and continue beating until stiff. Whip cream until stiff. Whip jelled coffee mixture until light and fluffy. Fold in egg whites first, then whipped cream. Spoon ¼ of mixture into a 2-quart serving dish or individual goblets, sprinkle with ¼ of almonds. Repeat layers three times. Chill at least 1 hour.

COLD PUMPKIN SOUFFLÉ

Photograph on page 109

Makes 8 servings

2 packages plain gelatin
1 cup C & H Golden
   Brown Sugar, packed
   Pinch of salt
4 eggs, separated
¾ cup milk

1 can (16 ounces)
   pumpkin puree
2 teaspoons pumpkin pie
   spice
1 cup whipping cream,
   whipped
   Finely chopped walnuts

Prepare 1-quart soufflé dish: Fold a band of aluminum foil long enough to fit around dish (double thickness and 4 inches wide).

Place around rim of dish to extend 2 inches above top. Fasten the ends securely with tape, string or straight pin.

Combine gelatin, half the sugar and the salt in top of double boiler. Set aside. Beat egg yolks and add to milk; stir into sugar mixture. Place over simmering water; stir until gelatin is dissolved. Remove from heat; stir in $\frac{1}{4}$ cup sugar, the pumpkin and spice. Cool until slightly thickened.

Beat egg whites until foamy. Gradually add remaining $\frac{1}{4}$ cup sugar and continue beating until stiff. Fold into pumpkin mixture. Fold in whipped cream. Pour into prepared soufflé dish. Chill at least 4 hours. Remove band. Press chopped nuts around edge of soufflé.

LEMON CLOUD

Makes 8 to 10 servings

1 cup C & H Granulated Sugar
4 eggs, separated
$\frac{1}{2}$ cup lemon juice
$1\frac{1}{2}$ teaspoons plain gelatin
$\frac{1}{4}$ cup cold water

1 teaspoon grated lemon rind
Pinch EACH salt *and* cream of tartar
Sweetened fruit

In top of double boiler, mix half the sugar, the egg yolks and lemon juice. Soften gelatin in cold water. Add gelatin to lemon mixture and cook, stirring, over simmering water, about 15 minutes, until mixture thickens. Stir in lemon rind. Cool, then chill until mixture begins to set.

Beat egg whites with salt and cream of tartar until soft peaks form. Beat in remaining $\frac{1}{2}$ cup sugar, 1 tablespoon at a time. Whip jelled lemon mixture until light and fluffy. Fold whites into lemon mixture. Chill at least 1 hour. To serve, scoop into serving dishes alternately with fruit.

CARAMEL CUSTARD

Makes 6 servings

1 cup C & H Granulated Sugar	⅛ teaspoon salt
2 cups milk	1 teaspoon vanilla
	5 eggs, slightly beaten

Pour half the sugar over bottom of 1-quart casserole or 8-inch square pan. Set 4 inches beneath broiler and broil 5 to 10 minutes, swirling pan occasionally, until sugar caramelizes and turns a deep mahogany brown. Cool 5 minutes.

Set oven to 325°F. Scald milk. Remove from heat before it boils and stir in remaining sugar, the salt and vanilla. Gradually mix in eggs. Pour into caramelized casserole. Place in pan of hot water (water should be ⅔ depth of casserole). Bring to simmer on top of stove, then bake 40 to 45 minutes or until custard is set and cake tester inserted into center comes out clean. Cool, then chill at least 4 hours. Unmold before serving.

HAWAIIAN COCONUT PUDDING

Makes 6 to 8 servings

1½ cups C & H Powdered Sugar	1 teaspoon vanilla
1 package plain gelatin	1⅓ cups flaked coconut
¼ teaspoon salt	2 cups whipping cream, whipped
1¼ cups milk	Sweetened fruit

In heavy saucepan, combine sugar, gelatin, salt and ¼ cup milk. When gelatin has softened, stir in remaining milk. Cook over medium heat, stirring constantly, until sugar and gelatin dissolve (do not boil). Stir in vanilla. Chill until mixture thickens enough to coat spoon. Fold in coconut and whipped cream. Pour into 6-cup mold. Chill 4 hours. Unmold and serve with sweetened fruit.

TWO-TONE COFFEE DESSERT

Makes 6 to 8 servings

²/₃ cup C & H Granulated
    Sugar
2 tablespoons instant
    coffee
1 cup milk

1 cup water
2 teaspoons plain gelatin
2 eggs, separated
    Pinch EACH salt *and*
    cream of tartar

In top of double boiler, mix ¹/₃ cup sugar, the coffee, milk and ³/₄ cup water. Soften gelatin in remaining water and add to mixture; heat over hot water. Beat egg yolks in small bowl. Gradually stir a little hot liquid into egg yolks, then pour yolk mixture into double boiler and cook, stirring, 5 minutes or until slightly thickened. Set aside. Beat egg whites with salt and cream of tartar until soft peaks form. Beat in remaining sugar, 1 tablespoon at a time; continue beating until stiff. Gradually fold hot mixture into meringue, mixing until smooth. Pour into individual dessert glasses and chill at least 2 hours (it will be set but not stiff).

FORGOTTEN TORTE

Makes 8 to 10 servings

6 egg whites, room
    temperature
¹/₄ teaspoon salt
¹/₂ teaspoon cream of
    tartar
1¹/₂ cups C & H Superfine or
    Granulated Sugar

1 teaspoon vanilla
¹/₂ cup whipping cream
    whipped with 1
    tablespoon C & H
    Powdered Sugar
    Berries, pineapple or
    other fruit

Preheat oven to 450°F. Grease bottom of 10-inch tube pan. Beat egg whites with salt and cream of tartar until soft peaks form. Beat in sugar, 1 tablespoon at a time, until stiff, glossy peaks form. Beat in vanilla. Spread evenly in pan. Put in oven and turn off heat immediately. "Forget" torte several hours, until oven is completely cold or overnight. Loosen edges and turn out onto serving plate. Chill. Meringue will keep at least 1 week in airtight container. No more than 6 hours before serving, frost with whipped cream. Chill. Before serving, decorate with fruit.

BLITZ MERINGUE TORTE

Almonds, whipped cream and your favorite fruit make this an unforgettable creation

Makes 8 to 10 servings

½ cup C & H Granulated Sugar

½ cup shortening

4 eggs, separated

3 tablespoons milk

1 teaspoon vanilla

1 cup cake flour or (1 cup all-purpose flour less 2 tablespoons)

1 teaspoon baking powder

¼ teaspoon salt
Pinch EACH salt *and* cream of tartar

¾ cup C & H Granulated Sugar

½ cup sliced almonds, toasted

1 tablespoon C & H Granulated Sugar

½ teaspoon cinnamon
Sweetened whipped cream
Sweetened fruit (fresh, canned or frozen)

Preheat oven to 350°F. Grease two 9-inch cake pans. Cream ½ cup granulated sugar and the shortening. Add egg yolks, 1 at a time, beating well after each addition. Stir in milk and vanilla. Combine flour, baking powder and ¼ teaspoon salt. Add to creamed mixture and beat until smooth. Pour into pans. Beat egg whites with pinch of salt and cream of tartar until soft peaks form. Beat in ¾ cup granulated sugar, 1 tablespoon at a time, until stiff, glossy peaks form. Divide meringue between pans, spreading over batter. Sprinkle with almonds, 1 tablespoon sugar and the cinnamon. Bake 30 minutes. Turn out onto rack to cool. No more than 6 hours before serving, place 1 layer, meringue side up, on serving plate. Spread with whipped cream and fruit. Top with remaining layer, meringue side up. Garnish with cream and fruit.

Blitz Meringue Torte with fresh raspberries

PEACHES-AND-CREAM CAKE

Makes 8 to 10 servings

1 cup C & H Granulated Sugar	1 teaspoon vanilla
½ cup (1 stick) butter or margarine, softened	1 tablespoon peach syrup
3 eggs	1 package (3 ounces) cream cheese, softened
1 cup all-purpose flour	¼ cup sour cream
1 teaspoon baking powder	Topping (recipe follows)
¾ teaspoon salt	

Preheat oven to 325°F. Cream ⅔ cup sugar and the butter. Beat in 2 eggs. Combine flour, baking powder and ½ teaspoon salt. Add to creamed mixture and beat until well mixed. Stir in vanilla and peach syrup. Spread evenly on bottom and sides of ungreased 10-inch pie pan.

Cream remaining ⅓ cup sugar with the cream cheese. Beat in sour cream. Add remaining egg and ¼ teaspoon salt; mix well. Spoon over batter in pie pan. Bake 30 to 35 minutes. Remove from oven and add topping.

Topping

1 can (29 ounces) cling peach slices	2 tablespoons C & H Golden Brown Sugar
½ pint (1 cup) sour cream	

Drain peaches (reserve 1 tablespoon syrup for cake batter). Arrange slices on top of cake. Blend sour cream with brown sugar. Spoon over peaches and return cake to oven for 5 minutes. Chill before serving.

Note: To substitute fresh peaches for canned, poach as follows: Combine 1 cup C & H Granulated Sugar, ½ cup water and 1 tablespoon lemon juice in heavy saucepan. Cook over low heat until sugar dissolves, swirling pan occasionally. Cover pan and cook 5 minutes. Peel 3 large peaches and slice ¼ inch thick. Add to sugar mixture, cover and simmer gently 3 to 4 minutes. Peaches should be tender when pierced with a knife. Cool in syrup. Proceed with topping recipe. Leftover syrup (canned or poaching) can be saved to top ice cream or other desserts.

HOT MILK SPONGE CAKE

Makes 8 to 10 servings

2 cups C & H Granulated Sugar
4 eggs
2 cups cake flour (or 1¾ cups all-purpose flour)
2 teaspoons baking powder

¼ teaspoon salt
2 teaspoons vanilla
1 cup milk
2 tablespoons butter
Mocha Frosting (recipe follows)

Preheat oven to 350°F. Cream sugar and eggs, beating until light and fluffy. Combine flour, baking powder and salt. Stir into creamed mixture, then beat well. Stir in vanilla. Heat milk and butter almost to boiling; quickly stir into flour mixture. Beat slightly. Pour immediately into ungreased 10-inch tube pan. Bake 40 to 45 minutes or until cake tester inserted in center comes out clean. Invert pan over bottle to cool. With long spatula, gently loosen cake from pan and turn out onto serving plate. Frost with Mocha Frosting.

Mocha Frosting

4 cups C & H Powdered Sugar
1 teaspoon instant coffee powder

3 tablespoons cocoa powder
⅓ cup butter, melted
1 teaspoon vanilla
4 to 5 tablespoons water

Sift sugar, coffee and cocoa in a bowl. Cream half the sugar mixture with butter. Stir in remaining sugar mixture, the vanilla and enough water to make a spreading consistency. Beat until smooth. Frosts two 8- or 9-inch layers.

ORANGE DELIGHT CAKE

Makes 8 to 10 servings

1½ cups C & H Granulated Sugar
½ cup butter or margarine, softened
1 teaspoon grated orange rind
2 egg yolks
2 cups cake flour (or 1¾ cups all-purpose flour)
2 teaspoons baking powder
¼ teaspoon salt
⅓ cup orange juice
½ cup water
4 egg whites, stiffly beaten
Orange Filling (recipe follows)
C & H Powdered Sugar (optional)

Preheat oven to 350°F. Grease and flour two 9-inch cake pans. Cream granulated sugar and butter until light and fluffy. Beat in orange rind and egg yolks. Combine flour, baking powder and salt. Add to creamed mixture alternately with orange juice and water, beating just until smooth. Fold in stiffly beaten egg whites. Turn into pans and bake 30 minutes or until cake tester inserted in center comes out clean. Cool in pans 10 minutes, then turn out onto rack to finish cooling. Spread Orange Filling on bottom layer, then stack. If desired, sprinkle top with powdered sugar or frost entirely.

Orange Filling

½ cup C & H Granulated Sugar
1 tablespoon butter
Grated rind of 1 orange
3 tablespoons orange juice
1 tablespoon lemon juice
2 egg yolks, beaten

In top of double boiler, combine sugar, butter, orange rind and citrus juices. Cook over direct heat until mixture reaches a boil, then place over hot water. Gradually stir in egg yolks, beating rapidly until mixture thickens. Cool before spreading between layers of cold cake.

SIMPLICITY LAYER CAKE

Makes 6 to 8 servings

1 cup C & H Granulated
    Sugar
$\frac{1}{2}$ cup butter or shortening
2 eggs, separated
2 cups cake flour (or $1\frac{3}{4}$
    cups all-purpose
    flour)
2 teaspoons baking
    powder

$\frac{1}{2}$ teaspoon salt
$\frac{1}{2}$ cup milk
$\frac{1}{2}$ teaspoon vanilla
$\frac{1}{4}$ teaspoon lemon extract
    Pinch EACH salt *and*
      cream of tartar
    Suntan Frosting (recipe
      follows)

Preheat oven to 350°F. Grease two 8-inch cake pans. Cream sugar and butter until light and fluffy. Add egg yolks and beat thoroughly. Combine flour, baking powder and salt. Mix milk, vanilla and lemon extract. Add dry ingredients and milk alternately to creamed mixture, beating well after each addition. Beat egg whites with pinch of salt and cream of tartar until stiff peaks form. Fold into flour mixture. Spread batter in pans and bake 30 minutes or until cake tester inserted in center comes out clean. Cool in pans 5 minutes, then turn out onto rack. Frost with Suntan Frosting.

Suntan Frosting

4 cups C & H Powdered
    Sugar
6 tablespoons C & H
    Golden Brown Sugar

5 tablespoons milk
3 tablespoons butter or
    margarine, softened
1 tablespoon vanilla
    Pinch of salt

Combine all ingredients in mixing bowl. Beat 2 minutes or until smooth and creamy. If too thick, add more milk, 1 teaspoon at a time. Frosts two 8- or 9-inch layers.

DELUXE ANGEL FOOD CAKE

Makes 8 to 10 servings

1 cup C & H Powdered Sugar
1 cup cake flour (or 1 cup minus 2 tablespoons all-purpose flour)
1½ cups egg whites (12), room temperature
1½ teaspoons cream of tartar
½ teaspoon salt

1 cup C & H Superfine Sugar
1 teaspoon vanilla
¼ teaspoon EACH lemon *and* almond extract
Rich Chocolate Sauce or Strawberry-Pink Angel Fluff (recipes follow)

Preheat oven to 350°F. Sift powdered sugar and flour together 4 times; set aside. Beat egg whites with cream of tartar and salt until soft peaks form. Beat in superfine sugar, 1 tablespoon at a time, until stiff glossy peaks form. Beat in vanilla and lemon and almond extracts. Gently fold in flour mixture, ¼ at a time, being careful not to deflate egg whites. Spoon lightly into ungreased 10-inch tube pan. With knife, cut through batter 5 times to break up large air bubbles. Bake 35 to 40 minutes on lower oven rack, until top springs back when gently touched. Invert pan over bottle to cool. With long spatula, gently loosen cake from pan and turn out onto serving plate. Frost, or serve with Rich Chocolate Sauce or Strawberry-Pink Angel Fluff.

Rich Chocolate Sauce

4 ounces (4 squares) unsweetened chocolate
2 cups C & H Powdered Sugar

½ cup evaporated milk or whipping cream
⅛ teaspoon salt
¼ cup (½ stick) butter or margarine

In top of double boiler, melt chocolate over hot water. Add sugar, milk and salt and beat until smooth. Add butter, cook 10 minutes longer, stirring occasionally. For a thinner sauce, add more evaporated milk. Serve warm, or refrigerate up to 1 week in covered container and heat over hot water before using.

Strawberry-Pink Angel Fluff

1 cup C & H Granulated
    Sugar
1 cup fresh strawberries*

1 egg white
Pinch of salt

Combine sugar, strawberries, egg white and salt in mixing bowl. Beat at high speed 10 minutes or until stiff peaks form.

*Note: Frozen strawberries may be substituted. Thaw and drain before measuring.

CHEESECAKE

Makes 12 servings

1 9-inch Graham Cracker
    Crust (see index)
2 packages (8 ounces
    each) cream cheese,
    softened

2 eggs
1½ cups C & H Powdered
    Sugar
1 teaspoon vanilla
1 pint (2 cups) sour cream

Prepare pie crust. Preheat oven to 350°F. Beat cream cheese until smooth. Add eggs, sugar and vanilla and mix thoroughly. Fold in sour cream and pour into prepared crust. Bake 30 minutes. Turn off oven. Leave cake in oven 60 to 90 minutes to cool. Serve cold.

Hint: What is the difference between a frosting and an icing? Probably none, but we've taken frosting to mean the covering and filling for cakes and icing to mean the frosting used for decorating.

DOUBLE CARAMEL CAKE

Makes 6 to 8 servings

1 cup C & H Brown
   Sugar, packed
½ cup shortening
2 eggs, separated
1½ cups cake flour (or 1¼
   cups plus 1
   tablespoon
   all-purpose flour)
1¾ teaspoons baking
   powder

¼ teaspoon baking soda
½ cup milk
1 teaspoon vanilla
   Pinch EACH salt *and*
   cream of tartar
   Caramel Frosting
   (recipe follows)
   Chocolate Curls (see
   index)

Preheat oven to 350°F. Grease and flour two 8-inch cake pans. Cream sugar and shortening until light and fluffy. Stir in egg yolks, 1 at a time, beating well after each addition. Combine flour, baking powder and soda. Mix milk and vanilla. Add dry ingredients and milk alternately to creamed mixture, beating gently after each addition. Beat egg whites with salt and cream of tartar until stiff but not dry. Fold into flour mixture. Spread batter in pans. Bake 25 minutes or until cake tester inserted in center comes out clean. Frost with Caramel Frosting and garnish with Chocolate Curls.

Caramel Frosting

½ cup (1 stick) butter or
   margarine
1 cup C & H Dark Brown
   Sugar, packed

¼ teaspoon salt
6 tablespoons milk
3 cups C & H Powdered
   Sugar

Melt butter in 2-quart saucepan; stir in brown sugar and salt. Bring to rolling boil and boil rapidly 2 minutes, stirring constantly. Remove from heat, stir in milk, then return to rolling boil. Cool 20 minutes or until lukewarm. Add powdered sugar and beat until smooth and cool enough to spread. If frosting stiffens too quickly while spreading, beat in several drops of milk. Frosts two 8- or 9-inch layers.

Double Caramel Cake with Caramel Frosting

OLD-FASHIONED BURNT SUGAR CAKE

Makes 8 to 10 servings

½ cup C & H Brown
Sugar, packed
½ cup boiling water
1½ cups C & H Granulated
Sugar
½ cup (1 stick) butter or
margarine, softened
2 eggs

2½ cups all-purpose flour
1 tablespoon baking
powder
½ teaspoon salt
1 cup milk
1 teaspoon vanilla
Burnt Sugar Frosting
(recipe follows)

Place brown sugar in heavy saucepan. Melt over low heat, swirling pan occasionally, until sugar caramelizes and turns a burnt, dark brown. Remove from heat and, at edge of pan, slowly stir in boiling water (stand back to avoid being splattered). Return to heat and boil mixture gently 5 minutes or until thickened. Cool.

Preheat oven to 350°F. Grease and flour two 9-inch cake pans. Cream granulated sugar and butter until light and fluffy. Stir in eggs, 1 at a time, beating well after each addition. Combine flour, baking powder and salt. Gradually add to creamed mixture alternately with milk, beating well after each addition. Stir in vanilla and 3 tablespoons cooled burnt sugar syrup (reserve remaining syrup for frosting). Pour batter into pans. Bake 30 to 35 minutes or until cake tester inserted in center comes out clean. Frost with Burnt Sugar Frosting.

Burnt Sugar Frosting

4 cups C & H Powdered
Sugar
⅓ cup butter or margarine,
softened

¼ cup reserved burnt
sugar syrup
1 teaspoon vanilla
3 to 6 teaspoons hot water

In large mixing bowl, combine all ingredients except hot water; mix well. Gradually stir in water, 1 teaspoon at a time, until good spreading consistency. Beat until smooth.

LIME CAKE

Makes 8 to 10 servings

1½ cups C & H Granulated
    Sugar
½ cup (1 stick) butter or
    margarine, softened
4 eggs, separated
½ cup lime juice
1½ teaspoons grated lime
    rind
1¼ cups all-purpose flour

½ cup cornstarch
4 teaspoons baking
    powder
½ teaspoon salt
    Pinch EACH salt *and*
    cream of tartar
    Lime Filling (recipe
    follows)

Preheat oven to 375°F. Grease and flour two 9-inch cake pans. Beat 1 cup sugar, butter, egg yolks and lime juice until light and fluffy. Stir in lime rind. Combine flour, cornstarch, baking powder and ½ teaspoon salt. Stir into creamed mixture. Beat egg whites with pinch of salt and cream of tartar until soft peaks form. Beat in remaining ½ cup sugar, 1 tablespoon at a time, until stiff. Fold into flour mixture. Pour into pans and bake 30 minutes or until cake tester inserted in center comes out clean. Turn out onto rack to cool. Fill layers with Lime Filling. Frost, if desired.

Lime Filling

1 cup C & H Granulated
    Sugar
2½ tablespoons all-purpose
    flour
¼ cup lime juice

1 tablespoon grated lime
    rind
1 egg
1 teaspoon butter

Combine all ingredients in small saucepan and cook over low heat, stirring constantly, until mixture boils. Cool before spreading between layers of cold cake.

Variation—Lemon Cake and Filling: Substitute lemon juice and rind for lime juice and rind.

PETITS FOURS

Makes 2½ to 3 dozen tiny cakes

California Pound Cake
(recipe follows)
Vanilla Buttercream
Frosting (recipe
follows)
Petits Fours Icing
(recipe follows)

1 teaspoon evaporated
milk (optional)
Food coloring
1 ounce (1 square)
unsweetened
chocolate

Bake California Pound Cake (or other firm-textured cake) in shallow pans. Remove from pans and place bottom side up on rack to cool. Spread bottoms of cakes with thin layer of Vanilla Buttercream Frosting; chill to set. Cut off side crusts and brush off crumbs. With knife or cutter dipped in warm water, cut cake into small squares, diamonds, circles or other fancy shapes. Arrange cakes ½ inch apart on wire rack set over cookie sheet.

Stir Petits Fours Icing over hot water until it reaches 105°F (slightly above body temperature). For extra gloss, stir in evaporated milk. Pour warm icing over cakes, tilting pan so that it flows in a wide sheath and completely covers tops and sides of cakes. Scrape up glaze that drips off; reheat by stirring over hot water to use again. (If necessary, thin with drops of hot water.)

After covering as many little cakes as desired with white icing, delicately tint remaining icing. Yellow coloring can be used for some, then the drippings made green with 1 or 2 drops of blue. Leftover colored icing can be reheated together, mixed with chocolate and used as chocolate icing.

Decorate tops of frosted cakes with buttercream frosting put through a decorating cone.

California Pound Cake

QE

4 cups C & H Powdered
  Sugar
1½ cups (3 sticks) butter or
  margarine, softened
6 eggs

3 cups cake flour (or 2½
  cups plus 2
  tablespoons
  all-purpose flour)
1½ teaspoons vanilla
¼ teaspoon salt

Preheat oven to 350°F. Grease and flour two 8-inch square pans. Cream sugar and butter. Add eggs, 1 at a time, beating well after each addition. Blend in flour, vanilla and salt. Pour into pans. Bake 15 to 20 minutes or until cake tester inserted into center comes out clean. Turn out onto rack to cool.

Vanilla Buttercream Frosting

Makes 2 cups—enough to frost two 8- or 9-inch layers

4 cups C & H Powdered
  Sugar
¼ teaspoon salt
¼ cup milk

1 teaspoon vanilla
⅓ cup (⅔ stick) butter or
  margarine, softened

Combine all ingredients in mixing bowl. Beat until smooth and creamy, frequently scraping down sides of bowl. If too stiff, beat in several drops of milk.

Petits Fours Icing

Glazes 30 to 36 Petit Fours

4 cups C & H Powdered
  Sugar
2 tablespoons light corn
  syrup

¼ cup hot water
1 teaspoon vanilla

Combine all ingredients and beat until smooth.

Note: Results are best if this recipe is prepared at least 24 hours (or up to 1 week) in advance and left to rest in cool spot.

127

STRAWBERRY JAM CAKE

Makes 8 to 10 servings

1¼ cups C & H Granulated
   Sugar
½ cup (1 stick) butter or
   margarine, softened
1 package (8 ounces)
   cream cheese,
   softened
2 eggs
¼ cup milk
1 teaspoon vanilla

2 cups cake flour (or 1¾
   cups all-purpose
   flour)
1½ teaspoons baking
   powder
¼ teaspoon salt
1 cup strawberry
   preserves or jam
Strawberry
   Buttercream Frosting
   (recipe follows)

Preheat oven to 350°F. Grease and flour 13x9-inch pan. Cream sugar, butter and cream cheese. Beat in eggs, milk and vanilla. Combine flour, baking powder and salt. Stir into creamed mixture. Spoon half the batter into pan, spreading evenly. Spread preserves over batter. Spoon remaining batter over preserves, spreading with spatula to cover preserves completely. Bake 35 to 40 minutes or until cake tester inserted in center comes out clean. Cool in pan, then frost with Strawberry Buttercream Frosting.

Strawberry Buttercream Frosting

4 cups C & H Powdered
   Sugar
½ cup (1 stick) butter or
   margarine, softened

¼ cup strawberry
   preserves
2 tablespoons milk
Pinch of salt

Combine all ingredients in large mixing bowl. Beat on low speed until blended, then beat on high speed 4 to 5 minutes until smooth, frequently scraping down sides of bowl. Frosts two 8- or 9-inch layers.

STRAWBERRY MERINGUE DELIGHT

Makes 6 to 8 servings

1 9-inch Meringue Shell
   (recipe follows)
2 cups C & H Powdered
   Sugar
½ cup (1 stick) butter or
   margarine, softened
3 egg yolks
1 tablespoon lemon juice

1 teaspoon grated lemon
   rind
1 pint fresh strawberries,
   hulled
½ cup whipping cream
1 tablespoon C & H
   Powdered Sugar
½ teaspoon vanilla

Prepare Meringue Shell and set aside to cool. Cream 2 cups sugar, the butter and egg yolks until light and fluffy. Beat in lemon juice and rind. Spread mixture over bottom of cold meringue shell. Top with berries. Whip cream with 1 tablespoon powdered sugar and the vanilla. Spread or pipe over fruit. Refrigerate 4 hours.

Meringue Shell

4 egg whites, room
   temperature
¼ teaspoon salt
½ teaspoon cream of
   tartar

1 cup C & H Granulated
   Sugar
½ teaspoon vanilla

Preheat oven to 275°F. Grease one 9-inch pie pan. Beat egg whites with salt and cream of tartar until soft peaks form. Beat in sugar, 1 tablepoon at a time, until stiff, glossy peaks form. Stir in vanilla. Spread meringue 1-inch thick on bottom of pan. Build up high fluffy border, keeping rim of pan free of meringue. Bake 1 hour or until meringue turns delicate cream color and feels dry and firm to touch. (It will crack while baking.) Cool in pan.

Variation — Individual Meringue Shells: On greased cookie sheet, divide meringue mixture into 6 or 8 mounds. With back of spoon, make cup-shaped hollow shell in center of each mound. Bake 1 hour or until meringues are creamy-white and delicately firm to the touch. Cool on rack.

STRAWBERRY-GLAZED CHEESE PIE

Makes 8 servings

1 9-inch Graham Cracker
  Crust (recipe follows)
½ cup C & H Granulated
  Sugar
1 cup large-curd cottage
  cheese, sieved
2 tablespoons flour
1 package (3 ounces)
  cream cheese,
  softened

3 eggs
¼ cup whipping cream
½ teaspoon grated lemon
  rind
1 tablespoon lemon juice
¼ teaspoon vanilla
⅛ teaspoon salt
  Strawberry Glaze
  (recipe follows)

Preheat oven to 325°F. Prepare Graham Cracker Crust. In large mixing bowl, combine remaining ingredients except Strawberry Glaze; beat thoroughly. Spoon into Graham Cracker Crust. Bake 1 hour. Cool, then top with Strawberry Glaze.

Graham Cracker Crust

Makes 8- or 9-inch crust

¼ cup C & H Granulated
  Sugar
2 cups graham cracker
  crumbs

½ cup (1 stick) butter,
  softened

Blend all ingredients and press firmly into 9-inch pie pan.

Strawberry Glaze

1 pint fresh strawberries,
  hulled
  Water

¾ cup C & H Granulated
  Sugar
2 tablespoons cornstarch

Reserve 1 cup of the prettiest strawberries. Mash remainder and press through sieve to eliminate seeds. Measure juice and add enough water to make 1 cup. Heat in small saucepan, then add sugar and cornstarch. Cook over low heat, stirring, until clear. Cool. Halve reserved berries and arrange on top of filling. Pour glaze over all. Chill until ready to serve.

Strawberry-Glazed Cheese Pie

TANGY LEMON PIE

Makes 6 to 8 servings

1 partially baked 9-inch
   Butter Pie Crust (see
   index)
1½ cups C & H Granulated
   Sugar
   Grated rind from 2
   lemons
⅓ cup lemon juice
⅓ cup water
6 eggs
1 large lemon
   Sweetened whipped
   cream

Prepare Butter Pie Crust. Preheat oven to 375°F. In bowl, mix sugar, lemon rind and juice, water and eggs. Pour into partially baked crust. Peel lemon, removing all white pith. Cut into thin slices with a serrated knife and remove seeds. Arrange lemon slices on top of filling. Bake 30 to 35 minutes until filling is puffed and browned and a knife inserted in center comes out clean. Serve hot or cold with whipped cream.

COFFEE CHIFFON PIE

Makes 8 servings

1 baked 9-inch pie crust
   (see index)
¾ cup C & H Golden
   Brown Sugar, packed
4 eggs, separated
¾ cup cold liquid coffee
1½ teaspoons plain gelatin
   Pinch EACH salt *and*
   cream of tartar
¼ cup C & H Granulated
   Sugar
1 cup whipping cream
2 additional tablespoons
   liquid coffee
¼ cup C & H Powdered
   Sugar

Prepare pie crust. In top of double boiler, mix brown sugar, egg yolks and ½ cup of the coffee. Soften gelatin in ¼ cup coffee. Add gelatin to sugar mixture and cook, stirring, over simmering water, about 15 minutes, until mixture thickens. Cool, then chill until mixture begins to set.

Beat egg whites with salt and cream of tartar until soft peaks form. Beat in granulated sugar, 1 tablespoon at a time; continue beating until stiff peaks form. Beat jelled coffee mixture until light and fluffy. Fold in whites. Turn into prepared pie crust and chill at least 1 hour until set. Before serving, combine cream, 2 tablespoons coffee and the powdered sugar. Whip until stiff and swirl over top of pie.

BERRY PUFF PIE

Makes 6 to 8 servings

1 9-inch Vanilla Crumb
   Crust (recipe follows)
4 egg whites
   Pinch EACH salt *and*
   cream of tartar
¾ cup C & H Granulated
   Sugar

½ teaspoon vanilla
2 cups sweetened berries
1 cup whipping cream
   whipped with 2
   tablespoons C & H
   Powdered Sugar

Prepare pie crust and set aside. Preheat oven to 325°F. Beat egg whites with salt and cream of tartar until soft peaks form. Beat in ¾ cup sugar, 1 tablespoon at a time; continue beating until stiff. Stir in vanilla. Spread in crumb crust and bake 40 minutes. Cool (filling will shrink as it cools). Spread berries over meringue, reserving several for garnish. Cover fruit with whipped cream and garnish with reserved berries.

Variation — Peach Puff Pie: Substitute 2 cups sliced peaches for the berries.

Vanilla Crumb Crust

1 cup vanilla wafer
   crumbs
2 tablespoons C & H
   Granulated Sugar

3 tablespoons butter,
   melted

Blend all ingredients. Press firmly over bottom and up side of 9-inch pie pan.

PUMPKIN PIE HAWAIIAN

Makes 8 servings

1 baked 9-inch pie crust
(see index)
²⁄₃ cup C & H Golden
Brown Sugar, packed
3 eggs, separated
¾ cup milk
1 package plain gelatin
1¼ cups pumpkin puree
1 teaspoon cinnamon
½ teaspoon allspice

¼ teaspoon EACH ground
ginger *and* nutmeg
Pinch EACH salt *and*
cream of tartar
½ cup C & H Granulated
Sugar
1 cup whipping cream
¼ cup C & H Powdered
Sugar
½ teaspoon additional
ground ginger

Prepare pie crust. In top of double boiler, mix brown sugar, egg yolks and ½ cup of the milk. Soften gelatin in remaining ¼ cup milk. Add gelatin, pumpkin, cinnamon, allspice, ¼ teaspoon ginger and nutmeg to sugar mixture. Cook, stirring, over simmering water, about 15 minutes, until mixture thickens. Cool, then chill until mixture begins to set.

Beat egg whites with salt and cream of tartar until soft peaks form. Beat in granulated sugar, 1 tablespoon at a time; continue beating until stiff peaks form. Without washing beaters, whip jelled pumpkin mixture until light and fluffy. Fold in whites. Turn into pie crust and chill at least 1 hour until set.

Before serving, whip cream with powdered sugar and ½ teaspoon ginger until stiff. Swirl over top of pie.

PERSIMMON CAKE ROLL

Makes 8 to 10 servings

1 cup C & H Granulated
  Sugar
4 eggs
2 tablespoons lemon juice
1 teaspoon grated lemon
  rind

1 cup all-purpose flour
1 teaspoon baking powder
¼ teaspoon salt
  C & H Powdered Sugar
  Persimmon Filling
  (recipe follows)

Preheat oven to 375°F. Grease a 15x10-inch pan and line with greased paper. Cream sugar and eggs about 6 minutes, until thick and lemon colored. Beat in lemon juice and rind. Combine flour, baking powder and salt and stir into egg mixture. Pour into pan. Bake 12 to 15 minutes. Loosen edges and turn out onto a towel sprinkled with powdered sugar. Remove paper; trim off crisp edges. Sprinkle cake with powdered sugar. Roll up in cloth; cool on rack. Unroll cake; spread with Persimmon Filling, leaving a ½-inch border on all sides. Reroll; place seam side down on serving plate. Sprinkle with powdered sugar.

Persimmon Filling

½ cup C & H Granulated
  Sugar
1 tablespoon lemon juice
3 medium-size ripe
  persimmons

1 cup whipping cream
¼ cup chopped pecans

Combine sugar and lemon juice in large heavy saucepan. Spoon pulp from persimmons, puree and add to pan. Cook over low heat until sugar dissolves, stirring occasionally. Raise heat to medium and continue cooking about 15 minutes, until mixture thickens enough to coat a spoon. When cool, beat whipping cream until softly whipped. Stir ¼ of cream into persimmon mixture and fold in the rest. Stir in pecans.

APPLE CRÊPE CAKE

Makes 8 servings

½ cup (1 stick) butter or margarine
8 large apples, peeled and sliced
1 cup C & H Golden Brown Sugar, packed
½ teaspoon cinnamon
¼ teaspoon nutmeg
Juice of 1 lemon
16 8-inch crêpes (recipe on page 138)
1 cup sliced almonds, toasted
Hot Caramel Sauce (see index)

Melt butter in large, heavy skillet. Add apples and toss carefully to coat with butter. Add sugar and sauté apples until just tender, keeping their shape as much as possible. Add cinnamon, nutmeg and lemon juice. Pour off any excess liquid. Reserve about 8 good slices for garnish.

On a heatproof serving platter, place a single crêpe, brown side up. Spread about 2 tablespoons of apple mixture over crêpe. Sprinkle a few almonds over apples. Repeat until all crêpes are used. Top with the reserved apple slices, making a pin wheel on top of the last crêpe. Cover with aluminum foil and heat in a low oven (225°F–250°F) until warm. Serve with Hot Caramel Sauce.

Note: To make larger Crêpes needed for this cake, use an 8-inch skillet.

From top: Crêpes (page 138) rolled with fresh fruit, Hot Caramel Sauce (page 25), Apple Crêpe Cake

CRÊPES

Photograph on page 137

Makes about 1½ dozen

2 tablespoons C & H Granulated Sugar	1 cup milk
½ cup all-purpose flour	4 eggs
Pinch of salt	5 tablespoons butter or margarine, melted

Combine sugar, flour and salt in bowl. Mix milk and eggs and gradually beat into sugar mixture, mixing until smooth. Chill at least 1 hour.

Stir in 3 tablespoons of the butter. Heat heavy 6½-inch skillet or crêpe pan. Brush with melted butter. Heat over medium-high heat until almost smoking. Remove pan from heat, ladle about 3 tablespoons batter into one corner of pan, then tilt pan in all directions until bottom is covered with a thin layer. Pour out any excess. Cook until bottom is lightly browned. Flip crêpe over and cook for about 1 minute until brown. Slide crêpe out onto plate. Repeat with remaining batter. Crêpes may be stored frozen up to 6 months. To freeze, place double layer of wax or plastic wrap between each cold crêpe. Place in plastic bag and seal.

CHESTNUT CREAM PUFFS

Makes 8 servings

1 tablespoon C & H Granulated Sugar	Egg wash (1 egg beaten with 1 teaspoon water)
¼ cup teaspoon salt	
¼ cup (½ stick) butter or margarine, cut into pieces	Chestnut Filling (recipe follows)
½ cup water	Chocolate Sauce (see index) or C & H Powdered Sugar
½ cup all-purpose flour	
2 large eggs	

Preheat oven to 450°F. Grease and flour cookie sheet. Combine sugar, salt, butter and water in medium saucepan. Bring to a rolling boil, remove from heat and add flour all at once, stirring hard. Return to heat and stir 1 minute with wooden spatula until mixture forms a ball and films the bottom of the pan. Cool 3 minutes. Add 1 of the eggs and beat until completely incorporated. Beat in remaining egg. Drop dough, 1 heaping tablespoonful at a time, in rounded mounds 2 inches apart on sheet. Brush tops of mounds with egg wash, being careful not to let mixture drip down sides of puffs or they won't rise. Bake 15 to 20 minutes until puffed and lightly browned. Reduce heat to 350°F and bake about 15 minutes longer, until crisp. Turn off oven. Cut a slit in the side of each puff and return to oven with door ajar to dry for 15 minutes. Cool on rack. Slice in half and sandwich with Chestnut Filling. Top with Chocolate Sauce or sprinkle with powdered sugar.

Note: If cream puffs are not served the day they are made, they should be frozen. Thaw and refresh for 5 minutes in a preheated 425°F oven. Slice, fill and serve.

Chestnut Filling

½ cup C & H Granulated
     Sugar
1 can (15½ ounces)
     chestnuts, drained
     and rinsed, or 2 dozen
     fresh chestnuts,
     cooked and peeled

¼ cup milk or cream
1 teaspoon vanilla
1 cup whipping cream

Combine sugar, chestnuts, milk and vanilla in blender or food processor. Puree until smooth. Whip cream. Stir ¼ of whipping cream into puree and fold in the rest.

CHOCOLATE CHARLOTTE RUSSE

Makes 8 to 10 servings

Ladyfingers (recipe
follows)
6 ounces semisweet
chocolate
½ cup (1 stick) butter or
margarine
6 egg yolks
¾ cup C & H Granulated
Sugar

⅓ cup water
2 cups whipping cream
2 tablespoons rum, crème
de cacao or orange
liqueur
Additional liqueur
Sweetened whipped
cream

Prepare Ladyfingers. Melt chocolate and butter together in top of
double boiler. Stir until smooth. Cool slightly at room temperature.
Beat egg yolks 10 minutes or until thick, lemon-colored and tripled
in volume. Combine sugar and water in small, heavy saucepan.
Cook over low heat until sugar dissolves, swirling pan occasionally.
Raise heat and cook until syrup reaches 236°F on candy thermometer (soft ball stage). Gradually beat sugar syrup into egg yolks. Stir
in melted chocolate mixture and continue beating until cool. Whip
cream and rum together. Stir about ¼ of cream into chocolate mixture to aerate, then fold in the rest.

Select a medium bowl or mold with narrow rounded bottom. Line
with foil. Sprinkle Ladyfingers lightly with additional liqueur. Using
as many Ladyfingers as necessary, arrange vertically around sides
of bowl with flat sides toward center, overlapping slightly. Fill with
half of chocolate mixture. Top with any remaining Ladyfingers.
Add remaining chocolate mixture. Cut off tops of Ladyfingers ex-
tending above chocolate mixture and arrange pieces on top of
chocolate filling. Cover bowl and chill overnight to set. Unmold and
invert onto serving platter. Decorate with sweetened whipped
cream.

Note: The arrangement of Ladyfingers will vary according to
mold. Use whatever is available and decorate as desired.

Ladyfingers

Makes about 1½ dozen

½ cup C & H Granulated
    Sugar
4 eggs, separated
⅔ cup all-purpose flour

Pinch EACH salt *and*
    cream of tartar
C & H Powdered Sugar

Preheat oven to 300°F. Line 2 large cookie sheets with parchment or grease and flour sheets. Beat granulated sugar and egg yolks until thick and lemon-colored. Fold in flour. With a clean beater in a different bowl, beat egg whites with salt and cream of tartar until stiff. Stir about ¼ of whites into yolk mixture; fold in the rest. Using a pastry bag with a ½-inch plain tube or a spoon, pipe out ¾-inch wide Ladyfingers 4 inches long. Sprinkle with powdered sugar. Bake 15 to 20 minutes, until lightly browned. Cool on rack.

Note: If you are using an unlined cookie sheet, allow the unbaked Ladyfingers to sit 5 minutes after sprinkling with sugar. Invert sheet and tap off excess sugar.

PEACHES IN RUBY SAUCE

Makes 6 servings

2 cups C & H Granulated Sugar	6 large peaches, peeled and halved
1 cup water	2 cups fresh raspberries (or two 10-ounce packages frozen raspberries, thawed)
1 tablespoon lemon juice	
½ teaspoon vanilla	

Combine sugar and water in large saucepan. Cook over low heat until sugar dissolves, swirling pan occasionally. Add lemon juice and vanilla. Cover pan and simmer gently 10 minutes. Add peaches, cover pan and poach 7 minutes (liquid should barely move) or until peaches are tender when pierced with a knife. Turn peaches halfway through cooking time. With slotted spoon, remove peaches to serving bowl.

If using frozen raspberries, drain syrup and add to peach liquid. Reduce syrup until thickened. Cool to lukewarm. Stir in raspberries. Pour over peaches. Chill until serving time.

Variation—Pears Cardinal: Peeled cored pears may be substituted for peaches in this recipe. Poaching time will be about 15 minutes.

6 CHOCOHOLIC'S CORNER

Any flavor—as long as it's chocolate

If you or a loved one is a chocoholic, here are a few tips that will insure your success with this delectable ingredient.

Three kinds of chocolate are used in cooking—unsweetened, semisweet and sweet. Cocoa used for making desserts should be unsweetened and the dark Dutch type.

Chocolate scorches easily and must be melted with care. There are several ways of doing this, but the basic rule is: melt chocolate with much liquid—or not a drop! For puddings, the chocolate may be melted with the milk and sugar. For some frostings and glazes, it can be melted with the shortening. For most baking, chocolate is melted alone and cooled before using. Melt it in a heavy-bottomed pan over low heat or, better still, in a heatproof dish set in hot water or in a double boiler over hot water. It may also be put in a low oven for 5 to 10 minutes or melted in a microwave oven.

Are you all set to make chocolate chip cookies and you have no chips? Cut up some semisweet chocolate instead. Remember that 1 package (6 ounces) chocolate chips equals 1 cup. If your recipe calls for ½ cup chips, cut up 3 squares of chocolate.

Many chocolate cake recipes call for buttermilk or sour milk—neither of which is a household standard (soured pasteurized milk should never be used). If you hate to buy a pint or quart when you need only 1 cup, try this magical alternative: place 1 tablespoon lemon juice or white vinegar in a measuring cup and add fresh whole milk to make 1 cup. Let the mixture stand 5 minutes and—presto!—1 cup of sour/buttermilk at your service. Before you tear your hair out over other missing ingredients, check the handy list of Substitutions on page 218.

Chocolate Curls as a garnish are as pretty as they are delicious. Use a vegetable parer and make long thin slices along the length of a bar of sweet chocolate. Use the curls to decorate cakes, puddings or pies. Melt 1 square of unsweetened chocolate with ¼ teaspoon of shortening and drizzle it around the edge of a white frosted cake. Or drizzle lines of chocolate across a white-frosted sheet cake. A knife drawn through the lines at regular intervals will leave a jagged decorative pattern.

Throughout this book, we've matched frostings to cakes, but they are all interchangeable according to your own taste. If you like extra-thick frosting or are switching to a different size cake which may require more, double the frosting recipe. Leftover frostings may be refrigerated in airtight containers up to 4 weeks and can be used in dozens of imaginative ways.

P.S. If you still crave chocolate after sampling the contents of this chapter, consult the index for even more of your favorite food—we love it too!

Chocolate Coconut Pie with Chocolate Coconut Crust (page 146)

CHOCOLATE COCONUT PIE

Photograph on page 145

Makes 8 servings

Chocolate Coconut
   Crust (recipe follows)
4 ounces unsweetened
   chocolate
1 cup C & H Powdered
   Sugar
½ cup (1 stick) butter or
   margarine, softened

Pinch of salt
1 teaspoon vanilla
3 eggs
1 cup heavy cream,
   whipped
Slivered orange rind

Prepare Chocolate Coconut Crust. Melt chocolate in double boiler over simmering water; cool. Cream sugar, butter and salt together until light and fluffy. Beat in vanilla and melted chocolate. Add eggs, 1 at a time, beating at high speed after each addition. Spoon into crust; chill. Top with whipped cream. Garnish with orange rind.

Chocolate Coconut Crust

2 ounces unsweetened
   chocolate
2 tablespoons butter
2 tablespoons hot milk

⅔ cup C & H Powdered
   Sugar
1⅓ cups coconut flakes

Grease 9-inch pie pan. Melt chocolate with butter in heavy saucepan. Remove from heat; stir in remaining ingredients. Mix well. Press firmly on bottom and sides of pie pan. Chill 1 hour before filling with chiffon filling, ice cream or cream filling such as the rich chocolate recipe above.

CHOCOLATE MOUSSE

Makes 6 servings

½ cup C & H Golden
   Brown Sugar, packed
¼ cup water
6 ounces semisweet
   chocolate pieces
4 eggs, separated
1 teaspoon vanilla

Pinch EACH salt *and*
   cream of tartar
1 cup whipping cream,
   whipped with 2
   tablespoons C & H
   Golden Brown Sugar
Sliced toasted almonds

Combine sugar, water and chocolate in top of double boiler. Heat over simmering water until chocolate melts, then beat until smooth. Cool slightly, then stir in egg yolks and vanilla. Beat egg whites with salt and cream of tartar until stiff peaks form. Fold chocolate mixture into egg whites. Spoon into individual serving dishes. Chill at least 3 hours to set. Before serving, top with sweetened whipped cream and almonds.

CHOCOLATE FUDGE PUDDING

Makes 6 to 8 servings

½ cup C & H Granulated
   Sugar
1 cup all-purpose flour
2 teaspoons baking
   powder
½ teaspoon salt
2 tablespoons cocoa
   powder
¾ cup chopped nuts
½ cup milk

1 teaspoon vanilla
2 tablespoons vegetable
   oil
¾ cup C & H Dark Brown
   Sugar, packed
¼ cup cocoa powder
⅛ teaspoon salt
1¾ cups hot water
Sweetened whipped
   cream

Preheat oven to 350°F. Grease 8-inch square baking pan. Combine sugar, flour, baking powder, salt and 2 tablespoons cocoa in bowl. Stir in nuts, milk, vanilla and oil. Spread in pan. Mix brown sugar, ¼ cup cocoa and salt; stir into hot water and pour over unbaked batter. Bake 40 to 45 minutes. As pudding bakes, batter rises through rich chocolate sauce. Serve warm or cold with whipped cream.

FUDGE NUT BROWNIES

Makes 2 dozen

1 cup C & H Golden
    Brown Sugar, packed
¼ cup (½ stick) butter or
    margarine, softened
2 eggs
2 ounces unsweetened
    chocolate, melted

1 teaspoon vanilla
¼ cup all-purpose flour
¼ teaspoon salt
1 cup coarsely chopped
    nuts
C & H Powdered Sugar

Preheat oven to 325°F. Grease 8-inch square baking pan. Cream sugar and butter until light and fluffy. Add eggs, 1 at a time, beating well after each addition. Beat in chocolate and vanilla, then add flour and salt. Stir in nuts. Pour into pan. Bake 30 minutes. Cool in pan; sprinkle powdered sugar over top; cut into bars.

COCOA BROWNIES

Makes 2 dozen

1 cup C & H Dark Brown
    Sugar, packed
2 eggs
1 teaspoon vanilla
⅓ cup vegetable oil
⅔ cup all-purpose flour

⅓ cup cocoa powder
½ teaspoon EACH baking
    powder and salt
1 cup coarsely chopped
    nuts

Preheat oven to 350°F. Grease 11x7 or 9-inch square baking pan. Gradually beat sugar into eggs and continue beating until thick and lemon-colored. Mix in vanilla and oil. Combine flour, cocoa, baking powder and salt and stir into batter; add nuts. Spread in pan. Bake 25 minutes. Cool in pan, then cut into bars or squares.

FROSTED BROWNIES

Makes 2 dozen

1 cup C & H Granulated
   Sugar
$^{1}/_{4}$ cup ($^{1}/_{2}$ stick) butter or
   margarine, softened
2 eggs
2 ounces unsweetened
   chocolate, melted
   and cooled

$^{3}/_{4}$ cup all-purpose flour
$^{1}/_{4}$ teaspoon salt
1 teaspoon vanilla
$^{1}/_{2}$ cup chopped walnuts
   Three Star Frosting
   (recipe follows)

Preheat oven to 350°F. Grease 8-inch square baking pan. Beat sugar and butter. Add eggs, 1 at a time, beating well after each addition. Stir in chocolate, then add flour, salt and vanilla; mix until smooth. Stir in nuts. Pour into pan. Bake 30 minutes. Cool. Frost and cut into bars.

Three Star Frosting

1 cup C & H Powdered
   Sugar
2 ounces unsweetened
   chocolate, melted
   and cooled

$^{1}/_{4}$ cup ($^{1}/_{2}$ stick) butter or
   margarine, softened
   Pinch of salt
$^{1}/_{2}$ teaspoon vanilla
2 tablespoons milk

Combine all ingredients and beat until smooth. Makes 1 cup

FUDGE CUPCAKES

Makes 2 dozen

1⅓ cups C & H Granulated
    Sugar
2 cups cake flour (or 2
    cups less 2
    tablespoons
    all-purpose flour)
2 teaspoons baking
    powder
1 teaspoon baking soda
½ teaspoon salt
½ cup (1 stick) butter or
    margarine, softened

¾ cup milk
2 teaspoons instant coffee
1½ teaspoons vanilla
½ cup milk
2 eggs
3 ounces unsweetened
    chocolate, melted
Chocolate Coffee Glaze
    (recipe follows)
Colored sugar crystals
    (optional)

Preheat oven to 375°F. Grease 24 muffin cups or line with paper baking cups. Combine sugar, flour, baking powder, soda and salt. Cream butter in large mixing bowl. Stir in dry ingredients. Combine ¾ cup of milk, the coffee and vanilla. Add to mixture and beat until smooth. Add remaining ½ cup milk, the eggs and melted chocolate. Mix until well blended. Fill muffin cups half full. Bake 20 minutes. Frost with Chocolate Coffee Glaze. Decorate with colored sugar, if desired.

Chocolate Coffee Glaze

2 ounces unsweetened
    chocolate
2 tablespoons butter or
    margarine

2 cups C & H Powdered
    Sugar
⅛ teaspoon salt
3 to 4 tablespoons strong
    liquid coffee

Melt chocolate and butter in double boiler over simmering water. Gradually beat in sugar, salt and enough coffee to reach a pouring consistency. Beat until smooth.

Top: Fudge Cupcakes with Chocolate Coffee Glaze, bottom: Chocolate Chip Cupcakes with Powdered Sugar Glaze (page 152)

CHOCOLATE CHIP CUPCAKES

Photograph on page 151

Makes 1 dozen

1 cup C & H Granulated
    Sugar
1 cup all-purpose flour
1½ teaspoons baking
    powder
½ teaspoon salt
½ cup semisweet
    chocolate chips

¼ cup (½ stick) butter or
    shortening, melted
1 teaspoon vanilla
2 eggs
    Milk (about ¼ cup)
    Powdered Sugar Glaze
    (recipe follows)
    Colored sugar crystals
    (optional)

Preheat oven to 375°F. Grease 12 muffin cups or line with paper baking cups. Combine sugar, flour, baking powder and salt in mixing bowl. Stir in chocolate chips. Melt butter in 1-cup measuring cup set in pan of hot water; cool to lukewarm, then add vanilla and unbeaten eggs; fill cup with milk. Add to dry ingredients and beat 3 minutes. Pour into muffin cups. Bake 20 to 25 minutes. Cool and frost with Powdered Sugar Glaze. Decorate with colored sugar, if desired.

Powdered Sugar Glaze

2 cups C & H Powdered
    Sugar
3 tablespoons milk, water
    or fruit juice

½ teaspoon vanilla

Combine ingredients and mix until smooth.

DEVIL'S FOOD LOAF

Makes 10 to 12 servings

3 ounces unsweetened
    chocolate
1½ cups C & H Superfine or
    Granulated Sugar
¾ cup shortening
3 eggs
1½ teaspoons vanilla
1 cup buttermilk

2¼ cups cake flour
    (or 1¾ cups plus
    ½ tablespoon
    all-purpose flour)
1 teaspoon EACH baking
    powder *and* baking
    soda
½ teaspoon salt
Easy Penuche Frosting
    (recipe follows)

Preheat oven to 350°F. Grease 12x8-inch loaf pan, three 8-inch cake pans or two 9-inch cake pans. Melt chocolate in top of double boiler over hot water; cool. Cream sugar and shortening until fluffy. Add eggs and beat thoroughly. Stir in chocolate. Add vanilla to buttermilk. Combine flour, baking powder, soda and salt. Add buttermilk and dry ingredients alternately to chocolate mixture, beating smooth after each addition. Pour into pan(s) and bake 40 minutes (loaf pan) or 25 to 30 minutes (8- or 9-inch layers). Cool on rack. Frost with Easy Penuche Frosting.

Easy Penuche Frosting

1 cup C & H Dark Brown
    Sugar, packed
6 tablespoons water
¼ teaspoon salt

6 tablespoons (¾ stick)
    butter or margarine,
    softened
4 cups C & H Powdered
    Sugar

Mix brown sugar, water and salt in saucepan. Stir over high heat until syrup comes to full rolling boil. Remove from heat immediately; add 2 tablespoons of butter. Cool 10 minutes or until bottom of pan feels lukewarm. Pour into bowl with powdered sugar. Mix together, then beat until smooth. Add remaining 4 tablespoons butter and beat until spreading consistency.

CHOCOLATE CREAM ROLL

Makes 10 servings

¾ cup C & H Granulated
 Sugar
4 eggs
1 teaspoon vanilla
½ cup all-purpose flour
⅓ cup cocoa powder
¼ teaspoon EACH baking
 soda *and* salt

2 cups heavy cream,
 whipped with ⅓ cup
 C & H Powdered
 Sugar
Chocolate Glaze (recipe
 follows)
Glacéed cherries and
 whole blanched
 almonds for garnish

Preheat oven to 400°F. Grease a 15x10-inch jelly-roll pan. Line
with greased waxed paper or parchment. Gradually beat sugar into
eggs and continue beating at high speed until thick and lemon-
colored. Beat in vanilla. Combine flour, cocoa, soda and salt and
gently fold into egg-sugar mixture. Spread batter evenly in pan.
Bake 10 to 13 minutes, until edges start to pull away from sides of
pan. Turn out immediately onto towel dusted with powdered sugar.
Peel off paper. Trim off crisp edges. Roll cake in towel (from short
side for pinwheel, from long side for log). Cool on rack. Unroll and
spread with whipped cream. Reroll (without towel) and place on
serving plate, seam side down. Top with Chocolate Glaze. Decorate with glacéed cherries and whole almonds.

Chocolate Glaze

1 tablespoon butter
1 ounce unsweetened
 chocolate
½ cup C & H Powdered
 Sugar

½ teaspoon vanilla
 Pinch of salt
1 to 2 tablespoons heavy
 cream or boiling
 water

Melt butter and chocolate in double boiler over low heat. Remove
from heat and stir in sugar, vanilla and salt. Stir in cream. Mixture
will be thick.

Chocolate Cream Roll with Chocolate Glaze

CHOCOLATE LAYER CAKE

Makes 8 to 10 servings

1¼ cups C & H Granulated Sugar	1 teaspoon baking soda
½ cup shortening	¾ teaspoon salt
2 eggs	1 cup water
1½ cups all-purpose flour	1 teaspoon vanilla
½ cup cocoa powder	Coffee-Rum
¼ teaspoon baking powder	Buttercream (recipe follows)

Preheat oven to 350°F. Grease and flour two 9-inch cake pans. Cream sugar and shortening. Add eggs, 1 at a time, beating well after each addition. Combine flour, cocoa, baking powder, soda and salt. Add alternately with water and vanilla to creamed mixture, beginning and ending with dry ingredients. Spoon into prepared pans. Bake 30 to 35 minutes. Cool on rack. Frost with Coffee-Rum Buttercream.

Coffee-Rum Buttercream

4 cups C & H Powdered Sugar	1 tablespoon rum (optional)
¼ teaspoon salt	⅓ cup (⅔ stick) butter or margarine, softened
¼ cup strong liquid coffee, cooled	

Combine all ingredients in large bowl; beat until smooth. If too stiff to spread easily, beat in more coffee a few drops at a time. Makes about 2 cups.

TRIPLE DECKER CHOCOLATE CAKE

Makes 15 to 18 servings

4 ounces sweet chocolate, chopped
½ cup boiling water
2 cups C & H Golden Brown Sugar, packed
1 cup (2 sticks) butter or margarine, softened
2 eggs

1 teaspoon vanilla
2¼ cups all-purpose flour
1 teaspoon baking soda
½ teaspoon salt
1 cup milk
Cocoa Fluff Frosting (recipe follows)

Preheat oven to 350°F. Grease and flour three 8- or 9-inch cake pans. Melt chocolate in boiling water. Set aside to cool. Cream sugar, butter and eggs. Add vanilla and melted chocolate; mix well. Combine flour, soda and salt. Add alternately with milk to chocolate mixture beginning and ending with dry ingredients. Pour into pans. Bake 35 to 40 minutes (8-inch) or 30 to 35 minutes (9-inch). Cool on rack. Frost with Cocoa Fluff Frosting.

Cocoa Fluff Frosting

4 cups C & H Powdered Sugar
¾ cup cocoa powder
¼ teaspoon salt
1 unbeaten egg plus enough water to measure ⅓ cup

1 teaspoon vanilla
¾ cup (1½ sticks) butter or margarine, softened

Combine sugar, cocoa and salt in bowl. Stir in egg, water, vanilla and butter and beat at moderately high speed 2 to 3 minutes or until thick and smooth. If too thick to spread easily, beat in a few drops of water. Makes about 2½ cups.

STEAMED CHOCOLATE PUDDING

An elegant yet comforting winter dessert

Makes 6 to 8 servings

¾ cup C & H Golden
    Brown Sugar, packed
¼ cup (½ stick) butter or
    margarine, softened
1 egg
1 teaspoon vanilla
3 ounces unsweetened
    chocolate
1¾ cups all-purpose flour

1 tablespoon baking
    powder
1 teaspoon EACH salt *and*
    cinnamon
1 cup milk
½ cup chopped walnuts
    Steamed Pudding Sauce
    (recipe follows)

Grease 2-quart mold. Cream sugar and butter. Add egg and vanilla; beat until smooth. Melt chocolate; cool. Stir into creamed mixture. Combine flour, baking powder, salt and cinnamon and add alternately with milk to chocolate mixture, beginning and ending with dry ingredients. Stir in walnuts. Spoon into mold and cover tightly with lid or heavy foil. Place on rack in large kettle. Add boiling water to come halfway up sides of mold. Steam 2 hours. Keep water boiling continuously. Add more boiling water as necessary. Let rest 10 minutes before unmolding. Serve warm with Steamed Pudding Sauce.

Steamed Pudding Sauce

1 cup C & H Granulated
    Sugar
½ cup light cream

½ cup (1 stick) butter or
    margarine
1 teaspoon vanilla

Combine all ingredients in saucepan. Heat until butter melts and sauce is hot. Pour over steamed pudding.

Steamed Chocolate Pudding with Steamed Pudding Sauce

BLACK FOREST CAKE

Germany's magnificent "Schwarzwalder Kirschtorte"
Makes 10 to 12 servings

Chocolate Sponge Cake
(recipe follows)
Poached Cherries
(recipe follows)
Chocolate Cherry
Frosting (recipe
follows)

1 cup whipping cream
2 tablespoons kirsch or
cherry liqueur
Chocolate Curls (see
index)

Prepare Chocolate Sponge Cake, Poached Cherries and Chocolate Cherry Frosting. Beat cream and kirsch together until softly whipped. With serrated knife, cut each cake layer in half horizontally to make 4 thin layers. Place first layer on serving platter, cut side up. Brush with cherry poaching syrup. Top with ⅓ of whipped cream. Place second cake layer on top. Brush with syrup. Mix drained chopped cherries with ¼ of Chocolate Cherry Frosting. Spread over second layer. Top with third layer, cut side up. Brush with syrup and cover with ⅔ of *remaining* whipped cream (reserve ⅓ for rosettes). Top with fourth layer. Frost top and sides with remaining Chocolate Cherry Frosting. With reserved whipped cream, pipe 10 to 12 rosettes through pastry tube around edge of cake top. Place reserved cherry on each rosette. Arrange Chocolate Curls in center of cake.

Chocolate Sponge Cake

1 cup C & H Granulated
Sugar
6 eggs, separated
1 cup all-purpose flour
¼ cup cocoa powder
1 tablespoon vanilla

2 tablespoons kirsch or
cherry liqueur
Pinch EACH salt *and*
cream of tartar
1 tablespoon C & H
Granulated Sugar

Preheat oven to 350°F. Grease and flour two 9-inch cake pans. Beat 1 cup sugar and the egg yolks until thick and lemon-colored. Combine flour and cocoa; quickly stir into sugar mixture on low speed, alternating with vanilla and kirsch. Beat egg whites with salt and cream of tartar until soft peaks form. Stir in 1 tablespoon sugar and beat until stiff. Stir ¼ of whites into batter, then gradually fold in the rest. Turn batter into pans. Bake 25 minutes or until cake tester inserted in center comes out clean. Cool in pans 10 minutes; turn out onto rack to finish cooling.

Poached Cherries

Also wonderful with sponge cake, pound cake, ice cream or meringue shells

½ cup C & H Granulated
    Sugar
¼ cup water
2 teaspoons lemon juice

1½ pounds tart or sweet
    cherries, pitted*

Combine sugar, water and lemon juice in small heavy saucepan. Cook over low heat until sugar dissolves, swirling pan occasionally. Raise heat to medium-high, cover pan and cook 5 minutes. Add cherries, cover and simmer gently 5 minutes. Cool in syrup. Drain, reserving both syrup and cherries. Set aside 10 to 12 cherries for garnish and coarsely chop remaining cherries.

*Note: If canned cherries are substituted for fresh when making Black Forest Cake, poaching is not necessary. Simply drain, reserve ½ cup syrup and proceed as directed.

Chocolate Cherry Frosting

¾ cup C & H Powdered
    Sugar
6 ounces semisweet
    chocolate, melted
    and slightly cooled

¾ cup (1½ sticks) butter or
    margarine, softened
2 egg yolks
2 tablespoons kirsch or
    cherry liqueur

Combine all ingredients; beat until smooth.

FUDGE CAKE

Makes 6 to 8 servings

2 ounces unsweetened
chocolate
3 tablespoons shortening
1 cup C & H Granulated
Sugar or 1 cup C & H
Golden Brown Sugar,
packed
2 eggs
½ cup milk

1 teaspoon vanilla
1 cup cake flour (or 1 cup
all-purpose flour less
2 tablespoons)
1½ teaspoons baking
powder
¼ teaspoon salt
Quick Fudge Frosting
(recipe follows)

Preheat oven to 350°F. Grease 9-inch round or 8-inch square baking pan. In mixing bowl, combine chocolate and shortening and set into larger bowl of hot water to melt; cool. When chocolate mixture is lukewarm, beat in sugar and eggs. Stir in milk and vanilla. Combine flour, baking powder and salt; add to chocolate mixture and beat until smooth. Pour thin batter into pan. Bake 25 minutes or until cake tester inserted in center comes out clean. Cool on rack. Frost with Quick Fudge Frosting.

Quick Fudge Frosting

4 cups C & H Powdered
Sugar
½ cup cocoa powder
¼ teaspoon salt

6 tablespoons boiling
water
1 teaspoon vanilla
⅓ cup (⅔ stick) butter or
margarine, softened

In mixing bowl, combine sugar, cocoa and salt. Mix in boiling water, vanilla and butter, then beat until smooth and thick. To speed thickening, set bowl in bowl of ice water while beating. If frosting stiffens too quickly while spreading, stir in a few drops of hot water.

DIANA'S CHOCOLATE SHEET CAKE

Makes 10 to 12 servings

2 cups C & H Granulated
 Sugar
2 cups all-purpose flour
1/3 cup cocoa powder
1 teaspoon baking soda
1/2 teaspoon salt
1 cup (2 sticks) butter or
 margarine

1 cup water
1/2 cup buttermilk
2 eggs
1 teaspoon vanilla
 Walnut Cream Frosting
 (recipe follows)

Preheat oven to 400°F. Grease and flour 15x10-inch baking pan. In large bowl, combine sugar, flour, cocoa, soda and salt. Bring butter and water to boil in saucepan and stir into sugar mixture. Beat in buttermilk, eggs and vanilla. Pour thin batter into pan. Bake 20 minutes. Frost while warm. Serve warm or cold.

Walnut Cream Frosting

4 cups C & H Powdered
 Sugar
1 cup chopped walnuts

1/2 cup (1 stick) butter or
 margarine
1/4 cup cocoa powder
6 tablespoons milk

In bowl, combine sugar and walnuts. Bring butter, cocoa and milk to boil in saucepan. Pour over sugared nuts. Mix; spread on hot cake.

163

COCOA APPLE CAKE

Tender, moist cake ... keeps well

Makes 10 to 12 servings

2 cups C & H Granulated
   Sugar
3 eggs
1 cup (2 sticks) butter or
   margarine, softened
¹/₂ cup water
2¹/₂ cups all-purpose flour
2 tablespoons cocoa
   powder
1 teaspoon EACH baking
   soda, cinnamon *and*
   allspice

1 cup minced nuts
¹/₂ cup semisweet
   chocolate pieces
2 medium apples, cored
   and grated (about 2
   cups)
1 tablespoon vanilla
   Chocolate Sour Cream
   Frosting (recipe
   follows)

Preheat oven to 325°F. Grease and flour 10-inch tube pan. Cream sugar, eggs, butter and water until fluffy. Combine flour, cocoa, soda, cinnamon and allspice; stir into creamed mixture. Fold in nuts, chocolate, apples and vanilla until evenly distributed. Spoon into pan. Bake 60 to 70 minutes or until cake tester inserted in center comes out clean. Invert pan and suspend over bottle until cool. With long spatula, gently loosen cake from pan and turn out onto plate. Frost with Chocolate Sour Cream Frosting.

Chocolate Sour Cream Frosting

3 cups C & H Powdered
   Sugar
²/₃ cup sour cream
   Pinch of salt
1 teaspoon vanilla

2 cups (12 ounces)
   semisweet chocolate
   pieces, melted and
   cooled

Beat sugar, sour cream, salt and vanilla until smooth. Beat in melted chocolate.

POTATO CAKE

Makes 10 to 12 servings

1¾ cups C & H Granulated Sugar
¾ cup (1½ sticks) butter or margarine, softened
2 eggs
1 cup cold mashed potatoes
2 ounces unsweetened chocolate, grated

1 cup chopped walnuts
2 teaspoons EACH baking soda, cinnamon *and* nutmeg
½ cup milk
C & H Powdered Sugar or sweetened whipped cream

Preheat oven to 350°F. Grease and flour 13x9-inch baking pan. Cream sugar and butter. Add eggs, 1 at a time, beating well after each addition. Mix in mashed potatoes, chocolate and nuts until well blended. Combine flour, baking powder, cinnamon and nutmeg. Add alternately with milk to creamed mixture. Spoon thick batter into pan. Bake 45 minutes or until cake tester inserted in center comes out clean. Cool. Sprinkle with powdered sugar or top with sweetened whipped cream.

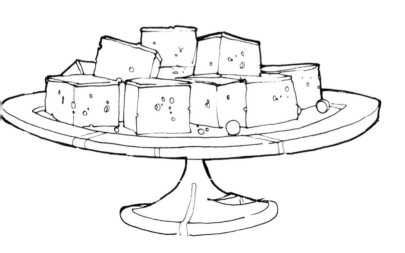

CHOCOLATE ALMOND TORTE

Makes 8 to 10 servings

1 cup sliced almonds,
   toasted
6 ounces semisweet
   chocolate
6 ounces butter or
   margarine
¾ cup C & H Granulated
   Sugar
4 eggs, separated
½ teaspoon almond
   extract or vanilla

¼ teaspoon salt
⅛ teaspoon cream of
   tartar
1 additional tablespoon
   C & H Granulated
   Sugar
Chocolate Almond
   Frosting (recipe
   follows)

Preheat oven to 350°F. Grease and flour 9-inch layer pan. Grind ½ cup of the almonds to fine meal; set remainder aside for decoration. Melt chocolate and butter together in top of double boiler. Stir until smooth. Cool to room temperature. Beat sugar and egg yolks together until thick, lemon-colored and tripled in volume. Beat chocolate into egg mixture. Stir in ground almonds and almond extract.

In separate bowl, with clean beater, beat egg whites with salt and cream of tartar until soft peaks form. Stir in 1 tablespoon sugar and continue beating until stiff but not dry. Stir about ¼ of egg whites into chocolate mixture to aerate and gently fold in the rest, being careful not to deflate the whites. Turn into pan. Bang lightly on counter to distribute batter evenly. Bake 30 to 35 minutes or until edges of cake are set and cake tester inserted in side of cake comes out clean (center will still be moist). Cool in pan 10 minutes, then turn out and finish cooling on rack. Cake will sink and crack as it cools. Smooth top of cake with spatula moistened in hot water. Frost with Chocolate Almond Frosting. Pat reserved sliced almonds around sides of cake.

Chocolate Almond Frosting

4 ounces semisweet
    chocolate
2 ounces unsweetened
    chocolate
1 cup C & H Powdered
    Sugar

¼ cup (½ stick) butter or
    margarine, softened
1 tablespoon almond
    liqueur, brandy or
    vanilla

Melt both chocolates in top of double boiler. Place in bowl with sugar, butter and almond liqueur; beat 5 minutes or until smooth.

CHOCOLATE DATE CAKE

Makes 8 to 10 servings

1¼ cups (8 ounces) snipped
    dates
1 cup boiling water
1 teaspoon baking soda
1 cup C & H Granulated
    Sugar
½ cup shortening
2 eggs
1 tablespoon grated
    orange rind

1 teaspoon vanilla
1¾ cups all-purpose flour
½ teaspoon salt
6 ounces semisweet
    chocolate pieces
½ cup chopped nuts
    C & H Powdered Sugar

Preheat oven to 350°F. Grease and flour 13x9-inch baking pan. Combine dates, water and soda; set aside until cool. Cream sugar and shortening. Add eggs, 1 at a time, beating well after each addition. Stir in rind and vanilla. Combine flour and salt; add alternately with date mixture, beginning and ending with dry ingredients. Stir in chocolate pieces and nuts. Spoon into pan. Bake 35 to 40 minutes. Cool. Sprinkle with powdered sugar.

CHOCOLATE TORTE

Makes 10 to 12 servings

¾ cup cake flour (or ¾ cup all-purpose flour less ½ tablespoon)
¼ cup cocoa powder
1 teaspoon baking powder
¼ teaspoon salt
4 eggs, separated
1 cup C & H Granulated Sugar

2 tablespoons water
1 teaspoon vanilla
Pinch EACH salt *and* cream of tartar
Cocoa Cream Frosting (recipe follows)
Chocolate Curls (see index)

Preheat oven to 375°F. Grease two 9-inch cake pans and line with greased paper. Combine flour, cocoa, baking powder and salt; set aside. Beat egg yolks and ½ cup of the sugar together until thick and lemon-colored. Mix in water and vanilla. Beat egg whites with salt and cream of tartar until soft peaks form. Add remaining ½ cup sugar, 1 tablespoon at a time, and continue beating until stiff peaks form. Alternately fold ⅓ of flour mixture and ⅓ of egg whites into beaten yolks until all are well blended. Spread batter in pans. Bake 20 minutes or until cake tester inserted in center comes out clean. Turn out on racks, peel off paper and cool. Split layers in half horizontally. Fill and frost sides and top with Cocoa Cream Frosting. Chill. Before serving, garnish with Chocolate Curls.

Cocoa Cream Frosting

1 cup C & H Powdered Sugar
2 cups (1 pint) whipping cream
½ cup cocoa powder

1½ teaspoons vanilla
Pinch of salt
2 teaspoons plain gelatin
2 tablespoons water

Combine sugar, cream, cocoa, vanilla and salt in bowl; chill. In small saucepan, soften gelatin in cold water. Cook over low heat, stirring constantly, until gelatin dissolves. Cool (about 5 minutes). Beat cream mixture until foamy. Add gelatin and beat until stiff. Keep refrigerated until ready to use.

7 EVERYBODY LOVES CANDY

Simple or fancy, it's easier than you think!

We all remember rainy afternoons spent making fudge or taffy and the exciting bustle of Christmas candymaking. Before the use of candy thermometers and stabilizers such as corn syrup and corn starch, candymaking was a chancey affair. Even the best of cooks didn't always get good results. But today it's easy to turn out a professional batch of candy—and it's still a lot of fun. For youngsters, candymaking is a wonderful introduction to the mysteries of the kitchen, but we suggest that little ones begin with our no-cook candies since accidents with boiling syrup can cause serious burns.

Temperature is the key to candymaking. A good candy thermometer is well worth its purchase price but if you don't have one and want to get started today, use the Cold Water Test chart on the next page. When reading your thermometer, be sure that the bulb is covered by the mixture but does not touch the bottom of the pan. Check the reading at eye level, even if you have to stoop. Watch carefully after the temperature reaches 220°F. Both humidity and altitude will cause temperature to vary. On rainy days, cook candies 2° higher than the recipe calls for and don't try to make hard candies on hot, humid days. To adjust for altitude, subtract 1°F for each 500 feet elevation above sea level. (If you don't know your altitude, simply place the thermometer in boiling water for 3 minutes. It should read 212°F; the difference is your altitude adjustment.)

Other rules to follow:
- Use a heavy, deep, straight-sided pan (3 to 4 quarts)
- Use wooden spoons for stirring

- Blend ingredients well before cooking, stir constantly until sugar dissolves and mixture is boiling. Add thermometer and stir occasionally to prevent burning
- Cook candy at a rather slow boil unless directed otherwise
- Wash sugar crystals off sides of pan with a clean pastry brush dipped in water, or a fork with the tines wrapped in a strip of dampened paper towel
- Pour candies from the pan, don't scrape. Scraping causes graininess

To insure creaminess, cool fudge to 110°F, or lukewarm, before beating or stirring. Don't worry if candy made with brown sugar and milk curdles while cooking. Beating will remedy this.

COLD WATER TEST

Remove pan from heat; drop ½ teaspoon boiling syrup into a cup of very cold water. Form ball with fingers; its firmness indicates temperature of syrup.

COOKING STAGE	COLD WATER TEST	TEMPERATURE (on candy thermometer)
Thread	Syrup spins a thread 2 to 3 inches long	230° to 232°F
Soft Ball (for fudge, penuche and fondant)	Syrup makes ball which can be picked up with fingers but will not hold its shape	232° to 240°F
Firm Ball (for caramels and caramel corn)	Ball will hold its shape when picked up	242° to 248°F
Hard Ball (for divinity and taffy)	Ball feels hard to the touch but is still plastic	250° to 268°F
Soft Crack (for toffee, butterscotch)	Syrup forms hard but not brittle threads rather than a ball	270° to 290°F
Hard Crack (for brittles, taffy apples)	Syrup forms brittle threads	300° to 310°F

Fudges: Uncooked Chocolate with almonds (page 172), Coffee with pecans (page 174), sliced Never-Fail (page 173), Creamy Chocolate Penuche with walnuts (page 174)

CHOCOLATE FUDGE

Makes about 2 pounds

3 cups C & H Granulated Sugar	2 tablespoons corn syrup
1¼ cups milk	¼ cup (½ stick) butter or margarine
4 ounces unsweetened chocolate or ½ cup unsweetened cocoa powder	1 teaspoon vanilla
	1½ cups coarsely chopped nuts

Grease 9-inch square pan. Combine sugar, milk, chocolate and corn syrup in 3-quart heavy saucepan. Stir over medium heat until chocolate melts and sugar dissolves. Wash down any crystals on sides of pan with brush dipped in cold water. Boil to 236°F on candy thermometer (soft ball stage). Remove from heat; add butter and mix by swirling pan, not by stirring. Set aside until lukewarm (110°F). Add vanilla and beat 10 to 15 minutes until candy thickens and begins to lose its gloss. Quickly stir in nuts and spread in pan. Cut when set.

 # UNCOOKED CHOCOLATE FUDGE

Photograph on page 171

Makes about 1 pound

3 ounces unsweetened chocolate	3½ cups C & H Powdered Sugar
¼ cup (½ stick) butter or margarine	1 egg
	2 teaspoons vanilla
	1 cup chopped nuts

Line 8-inch square pan with waxed paper. In heavy saucepan, melt chocolate and butter over low heat. Stir half the sugar into chocolate mixture, then beat in egg and vanilla. Gradually work in remaining sugar. Add nuts. Press into pan. Let set until firm, then turn out and cut into squares.

NEVER-FAIL FUDGE

Photograph on page 171

Makes about 1 pound

2 cups C & H Powdered Sugar	2 ounces unsweetened chocolate
3 ounces cream cheese	½ cup chopped nuts
⅛ teaspoon salt	1 teaspoon whipping cream (optional)
½ teaspoon vanilla	

Gradually stir sugar into cream cheese. Add salt and vanilla. Melt chocolate in top of double boiler, cool slightly and stir into cheese mixture. Add nuts. For softer fudge, add cream. Press into well-greased shallow pan or roll into log. Chill until firm; cut when set.

CLASSIC COCOA FUDGE

How long has it been since the whole family gathered in the kitchen to make candy?

Makes about 36 pieces

3 cups C & H Granulated Sugar	1½ cups milk
⅔ cup cocoa powder	¼ cup (½ stick) butter or margarine
⅛ teaspoon salt	1 teaspoon vanilla

Lightly grease 8- or 9-inch square pan. Combine sugar, cocoa and salt in heavy 4-quart saucepan; stir in milk. Bring to rolling boil on medium heat, stirring constantly. Continue boiling until mixture reaches 236°F on candy thermometer (soft ball stage). Remove from heat. Add butter and vanilla; mix by swirling pan, not by stirring. Cool until lukewarm (110°F). Beat with wooden spoon until fudge loses its gloss. Spread quickly in pan. Cut when set.

Variation—Marshmallow Nut Fudge: Increase cocoa to ¾ cup. Cook fudge as above. Add 1 cup marshmallow cream with butter and vanilla; mix by swirling pan. Cool to lukewarm (110°F). Beat 10 minutes; stir in 1 cup broken nuts and pour into pan. (Fudge will not set until it is poured into pan.) Cut when set.

COFFEE FUDGE

Photograph on page 171

Makes about 2½ pounds

3 cups C & H Granulated or Superfine Sugar
2 tablespoons instant coffee
1 cup milk
¼ cup cream
2 tablespoons corn syrup
¼ cup (½ stick) butter or margarine
1 teaspoon vanilla
1½ cups coarsely chopped pecans

Combine sugar, coffee, milk, cream and corn syrup in heavy saucepan. Stir over low heat until mixture begins to boil. Cook until it reaches 236°F on candy thermometer (soft ball stage). Wash down any sugar crystals on sides of pan with brush dipped in cold water. Stir frequently to prevent scorching. Pour into clean bowl to prevent graininess, stir in butter and cool to lukewarm (110°F) without stirring. Stir in vanilla, then beat 10 to 15 minutes until fudge loses its gloss. Stir in pecans, beat until candy holds its shape. Drop from teaspoon onto greased cookie sheet or waxed paper to set.

CREAMY CHOCOLATE PENUCHE

Photograph on page 171

Makes about 1¼ pounds

2 cups C & H Granulated Sugar
1 cup half-and-half
2 ounces unsweetened chocolate
2 tablespoons light corn syrup
½ teaspoon salt
2 tablespoons butter, cut into 6 pieces
1 teaspoon vanilla
½ cup coarsely chopped walnuts

Grease 8-inch square pan. Combine sugar, half-and-half, chocolate, corn syrup and salt in heavy saucepan. Stir over medium heat until mixture begins to boil. Cook until it reaches 236°F on candy thermometer (soft ball stage). Wash down any crystals on sides of pan with brush dipped in cold water. Stir frequently to prevent scorching. Pour into clean bowl to prevent graininess. Stir in butter and vanilla, cool to lukewarm (110°F) without stirring. Beat 10 to 15 minutes until fudge thickens and begins to lose its gloss. Quickly stir in walnuts and spread in pan. Cool and cut into squares.

CREAM FONDANT

Makes about 1 1/4 pounds

3 cups C & H Granulated Sugar	1 tablespoon light corn syrup
1 1/2 cups water	Pinch of cream of tartar

Combine sugar, water, corn syrup and cream of tartar in saucepan. Cook over low heat until sugar dissolves, then raise heat and boil until mixture reaches 236°F on candy thermometer (soft ball stage). Wash down any crystals on sides of pan with brush dipped in cold water. Immediately pour onto wet marble slab or porcelain tabletop to cool. When lukewarm, scrape fondant with scraper or wooden spoon toward center of slab. Continue lifting and folding until fondant is creamy and stiff. Knead until smooth. Place in covered container and store in cool place to ripen for 24 hours. Fondant may be stored up to 2 weeks.

When ready to use, reheat fondant in double boiler, fondue pot or chafing dish, stirring constantly so it will melt evenly. When lukewarm (110°F), use fork, toothpicks or skewers to dip fruits or nuts into fondant. Try almonds, dates, raisins, strawberries or fresh pitted cherries. Place on waxed paper to firm.

Variation — Chocolate Covered Cherries: Coat pitted cherries with fondant and chill until firm. Melt 1 to 2 pounds grated dipping chocolate in top of double boiler and stir over hot water (not boiling) until mixture reaches 85°F or a drop feels lukewarm on bottom lip. Do not heat over 110°F. With knife, put a bit of chocolate on bottom of each fondant-coated cherry. Place on waxed paper to harden, then coat entire cherry by submerging in chocolate. Remove with fork and place on waxed paper to set. (This double chocolate coating on the bottom keeps candy from leaking. After standing a few days, the fondant will become liquid.)

SALT WATER TAFFY

The next time your daughter has a sleep-in, suggest making this candy as the evening's entertainment

Makes about 2 pounds

2 cups C & H Granulated Sugar
1¼ cups light corn syrup
1 cup water
1 teaspoon salt
2 tablespoons butter

Food coloring and flavoring
4 tablespoons C & H Powdered Sugar
2 tablespoons cornstarch

In large heavy saucepan, combine granulated sugar, corn syrup and water. Place over high heat, stirring constantly until it boils. Reduce heat to medium and continue cooking until it reaches 260°F on candy thermometer (hard ball stage). Remove from heat; add salt and butter. Pour into a buttered 15x10-inch pan. When cool (about 20 minutes), knead coloring and flavoring into candy, then slowly pull candy until hands are 18 inches apart. Fold in half and continue pulling and folding 20 to 30 minutes until candy is hard. Candy will look smooth and satin-like. Shape into rope about ½ inch thick. Cut rope into bite-size pieces and drop on surface that has been dusted with a mixture of powdered sugar and cornstarch. Wrap individually in waxed paper; store in airtight containers. Taffy should remain chewy for one week.

Variation — Molasses Salt Water Taffy: For C & H Granulated Sugar, substitute packed C & H Brown Sugar.

Salt Water Taffy (Peppermint and Molasses)

PEANUT BRITTLE

This American favorite is easy to make, hard to resist

Makes about 2 pounds

2 cups salted peanuts	¾ cup light corn syrup
2 cups C & H Golden Brown Sugar, packed	2 tablespoons butter
½ cup water	½ teaspoon vanilla
	1 teaspoon baking soda

Spread peanuts in shallow pan and place in 200°F oven. In 3-quart saucepan, combine sugar, water and syrup. Cook over medium heat, stirring constantly, until sugar dissolves, then raise heat and cook until mixture reaches 295°F on candy thermometer (hard crack stage). Wash down any crystals on sides of pan with brush dipped in cold water. Swirl pan frequently so mixture doesn't burn. Stir in butter, then hot peanuts and vanilla. Remove from heat and add soda immediately, stirring rapidly until light and foamy. Quickly pour onto well-oiled marble slab or 2 large cookie sheets, spreading into a thin layer. When brittle begins to set, loosen and flip it over. Stretch as thin as possible. Let cool, then break into pieces. Store tightly covered.

OLDE ENGLISH TOFFEE

Cheers to the British for this elegant version of our peanut brittle

Makes about 1¼ pounds

1 cup chopped roasted unblanched almonds	⅓ cup C & H Brown Sugar, packed
1 cup (2 sticks) butter or margarine	2 tablespoons water
1 cup C & H Granulated Sugar	½ teaspoon baking soda
	3 ounces semisweet chocolate pieces

Sprinkle half the almonds in a 13x9-inch pan. In 3-quart saucepan, melt butter; add sugars and water. Stir constantly until mixture reaches a boil. Continue boiling until it reaches 300°F on candy thermometer (hard crack stage). Swirl pan occasionally to prevent burning. Working quickly, remove from heat, stir in soda and spread mixture carefully over almonds. Cool 5 minutes. Sprinkle chocolate pieces over toffee, spreading evenly with spatula as heat melts it. Sprinkle remaining almonds over chocolate and press in lightly. Cool. Break into pieces.

DIVINITY

How can one teaspoon of powdered sugar make such a flavor and texture difference?

Makes about 50 pieces

2 cups C & H Granulated Sugar
½ cup light corn syrup
½ cup water
⅛ teaspoon salt
2 egg whites
Pinch EACH salt *and* cream of tartar

1 teaspoon vanilla
1 teaspoon C & H Powdered Sugar
½ cup coarsely chopped nuts (optional)

Combine granulated sugar, corn syrup, water and ⅛ teaspoon salt in saucepan and cook over low heat until sugar dissolves. Raise heat and cook until mixture reaches 260°F on candy thermometer (hard ball stage). Wash down any crystals on sides of pan with brush dipped in cold water. Swirl pan occasionally so mixture doesn't burn. Meanwhile, add pinch of salt and cream of tartar to egg whites and beat until stiff. Gradually pour hot syrup into whites, beating constantly, until candy begins to hold its shape. Beat in vanilla, powdered sugar and nuts. Drop from teaspoon onto waxed paper or buttered cookie sheet. Let rest several hours until firm. Store in airtight container.

Hint: When color is not important, light and dark syrups may be used interchangeably. When color is important, the type to be used is specified.

NO-COOK CANDY ROLL

Makes 40 pieces

¼ cup (½ stick) butter or margarine	2 tablespoons glacéed cherries, chopped
¼ cup evaporated milk	1 ounce unsweetened chocolate, melted
1 teaspoon vanilla	Minced nuts
¼ teaspoon salt	
4 cups C & H Powdered Sugar	

Melt butter in saucepan. Stir in milk, vanilla and salt. Remove from heat and gradually stir in sugar. Mix well. Measure ½ cup mixture into small bowl. Add cherries and mix well. Work melted chocolate into remaining mixture. Knead with hands until smooth and blended. If chocolate mixture is dry, add evaporated milk by ½ teaspoonfuls until desired consistency is reached.

Divide in half. Roll each piece between waxed paper. Cut to 5x10-inch rectangles. Divide cherry candy in half and form into 2 rolls, each 10 inches long. Lay each on chocolate and roll up, then roll in minced nuts. Seal in foil. Refrigerate 1 hour or until ready to slice. Slice ½ inch thick. With leftover chocolate, make 1-inch balls and roll in nuts.

COCONUT JOYS

Makes about 36 pieces

2 cups C & H Powdered Sugar	½ cup (1 stick) butter or margarine, melted
3 cups (8 ounces) flaked coconut	2 ounces unsweetened chocolate, melted

Combine sugar, coconut and butter; beat until well mixed. Shape rounded teaspoons of candy mixture into balls and arrange on cookie sheet. Make an indentation in center of each candy and fill with melted chocolate. Chill until firm. Store in refrigerator.

Foreground left to right: Opera Nut Creams (page 182), Crystallized Nuts (page 185) and No-Cook Candy Roll

OPERA NUT CREAMS

Photograph on page 181

Makes 2 pounds

2 cups C & H Granulated
    Sugar
³⁄₄ cup whipping cream
¹⁄₂ cup milk
1 tablespoon light corn
    syrup

¹⁄₈ teaspoon salt
1 teaspoon vanilla
³⁄₄ cup chopped walnuts
6 ounces semisweet
    chocolate, melted
Fruit or nuts (optional)

Grease 8-inch square pan. Combine sugar, cream, milk, corn syrup and salt in 4-quart saucepan (candy needs room to foam while boiling). Bring to boil over medium heat and cook until it reaches 236°F on a candy thermometer (soft ball stage). Remove from heat and cool to lukewarm (110°F) without stirring. Add vanilla and beat until mixture loses its gloss. Stir in nuts and spoon into pan. Cool until firm, then spread melted chocolate over top. Cool again and cut into squares. Garnish, if desired, with fruit or nuts.

CHOCOLATE NUT CANDY

An unusual (unusually delicious!) homemade confection

Makes about 1 pound

2 egg yolks
1 cup milk
¹⁄₂ cup C & H Granulated
    Sugar
¹⁄₂ cup flour
Pinch of salt

7 ounces semisweet
    chocolate pieces
1 tablespoon butter or
    margarine
1 teaspoon vanilla
1¹⁄₂ cups minced walnuts

In top of double boiler, beat egg yolks and milk together. Combine sugar, flour and salt and stir into egg mixture. Place over hot water and cook, stirring briskly, 5 minutes or until very thick. Remove from hot water, add chocolate, butter and vanilla. Stir until chocolate melts. Cool, stirring occasionally, then drop 1 teaspoonful at a time into chopped nuts; roll in nuts. Store in refrigerator.

HAZELNUT ORANGE TRUFFLES

These small bonbons are called "truffles" because they look just like the French delicacy

Makes about 20 pieces

Hazelnut Praline
(recipe follows)
8 ounces semisweet
chocolate pieces
6 tablespoons (3/4 stick)
butter or margarine,
cut into 12 pieces

2 tablespoons orange
liqueur or liquid coffee
C & H Powdered Sugar
Cocoa powder

Prepare Hazelnut Praline. Combine chocolate and butter in top of double boiler and melt over simmering water, stirring occasionally until smooth. Strain through fine sieve. Cool at room temperature. Stir in orange liqueur and chopped Hazelnut Praline. Refrigerate 4 hours or until firm. Scoop out truffle mixture with spoon or melon baller and roll into 1-inch balls. Place half of truffles in bowl of powdered sugar and half in bowl of cocoa. Shake bowls until truffles are well coated. Arrange in individual fluted candy papers and store in closed container. Truffles will keep several weeks in refrigerator. Before serving, leave in closed container at room temperature for 15 minutes.

Hazelnut Praline

1/2 cup hazelnuts, Brazil
nuts or almonds

1/2 cup C & H Granulated
Sugar
1/4 cup water

Preheat oven to 300°F. Toast hazelnuts 15 to 20 minutes until brown. Rub between palms, in towel or in sieve to remove husks. Grease cookie sheet. Combine sugar and water in small heavy saucepan. Cook over low heat until sugar dissolves, swirling pan occasionally. Raise heat and boil until sugar caramelizes. Wash down any sugar crystals on sides of pan with brush dipped in cold water. Stir in hazelnuts. Pour onto tray. Chop coarsely when hard.

CARAMEL APPLES

Gloriously sweet and gooey reminders of childhood

Makes 6 caramel apples

1 cup C & H Golden
   Brown Sugar, packed
½ cup C & H Granulated
   Sugar
½ cup light corn syrup
½ cup water
1 tablespoon butter or
   margarine

1 teaspoon vanilla
6 crisp medium-sized
   apples, stems
   removed
6 wooden skewers or
   popsicle sticks

Grease cookie sheet. In saucepan, combine sugars, corn syrup and water. Cook over low heat until sugars are dissolved, shaking pan occasionally. Raise heat and cook, without stirring, until mixture reaches 270°F on candy thermometer (soft crack stage). Stir in butter and vanilla, then remove from heat. Insert skewer in stem end of each apple and turn in syrup until completely coated. Remove quickly and stand on cookie sheet to cool.

 # SUGARED WALNUTS

Perfect finishing touch for a plate of homemade candies

Makes about 4 cups

1 cup C & H Golden
   Brown Sugar, packed
½ cup water
½ teaspoon salt

2 teaspoons cinnamon
½ teaspoon EACH ground
   cloves *and* nutmeg
2 cups walnut halves

Combine sugar, water, salt, cinnamon, cloves and nutmeg in heavy saucepan. Place on high heat, stirring constantly, until mixture boils. Continue boiling until it reaches 236°F on candy thermometer (soft ball stage), stirring occasionally to prevent burning. Remove from heat. Stir in walnuts. Continue stirring 3 to 6 minutes until creamy. Turn out on waxed paper; separate walnuts using 2 forks. Cool.

CHOCOLATE CREAMS

Makes about 60 small creams

½ cup (1 stick) butter or margarine

3 ounces semisweet chocolate pieces

1 teaspoon vanilla

1 tablespoon cream or evaporated milk

4 cups C & H Powdered Sugar

1 egg white, stiffly beaten

Melt butter and chocolate in top of double boiler over hot water. Add vanilla and cream. Gradually beat in half the sugar, fold in beaten egg white. Add remaining sugar, beating until smooth. Working quickly, drop by teaspoonfuls onto waxed paper. (Keep pan over hot water; stir often. If candy hardens too quickly in pan, add a few drops of cream.) Chill several hours until firm. Store in refrigerator with waxed paper between layers.

Variation — Minty Chocolate Creams: Stir in 1 teaspoon mint extract instead of vanilla.

Variation — Coffee Creams: Stir in 1 tablespoon instant coffee after butter is melted. Omit chocolate, if desired.

CRYSTALLIZED NUTS

Photograph on page 181

Makes about 1½ pounds

1¼ cups C & H Golden Brown Sugar, packed

¼ cup cream

1 tablespoon butter or margarine

½ teaspoon cinnamon

⅛ teaspoon salt

1 teaspoon vanilla

2 cups whole blanched almonds

Combine sugar, cream, butter, cinnamon and salt in 2-quart saucepan. Bring to boil over medium heat and continue cooking, stirring constantly, until mixture reaches 224°F on candy thermometer (firm ball stage). Remove from heat. Add vanilla and nuts and stir until candy grains on nuts. Spread on cookie sheet to cool.

185

CANDIED RIND

Makes about 8 dozen

2 grapefruits or 3 oranges
    or 6 lemons
½ teaspoon salt
1 cup C & H Granulated
    Sugar

¾ cup water
2 tablespoons light corn
    syrup
Additional C & H
    Granulated Sugar

Remove rind in large pieces or use rind from fruit that has been squeezed for juice. Cover rind with cold water; add salt and boil, uncovered, for 20 minutes. Drain and rinse. Cover with fresh water and boil 15 minutes; drain well. With spoon scrape out any ragged membranes. Cut rind into thin strips. In large saucepan, mix sugar, water and syrup. Bring to a boil; add rind. Boil gently, stirring often, until most of syrup is absorbed. Drain a few pieces at a time; roll in sugar. Spread on waxed paper to dry. Store tightly covered.

CRYSTALLIZED GINGER

Chop and mix with cream cheese, sandwich with orange bread

Makes 1 cup

4 ounces gingerroot
½ cup C & H Granulated
    Sugar

¼ cup water
    C & H Granulated
    Sugar

Wash and scrape ginger. Cut against grain into ⅛-inch-thick slices. You should have about 1 cup. In a saucepan, cover ginger with cold water; bring to boil and boil 5 minutes. Drain. Repeat draining and boiling process until root is tender. Drain on paper towels 30 minutes.

Combine sugar and ¼ cup water in heavy 1½-quart saucepan. Place over low heat until sugar is dissolved, shaking pan occasionally; then raise heat and boil gently 5 minutes. Add ginger slices; stir until boiling. Cook about 25 minutes until syrup is absorbed, stirring occasionally to prevent burning. Place on rack to dry partially. Roll in sugar.

8 STORING UP SUNSHINE

Preserve summer fruits to brighten winter days

Making jellies, jams and other goodies that will store up the taste of summer during cheerless winter months is easy enough if you follow a few simple rules and have the proper equipment on hand.

In general, all preserves should be made in small amounts (about 4 cupfuls of fruit) and recipes never doubled. An 8- to 10-quart heavy kettle with a large, flat bottom allows the preserves to boil quickly and evenly. To sterilize glasses and jars, place a folded dish towel in the bottom of a deep pot and place the containers on it. Glasses and jars that are not nicked may be reused, but the lids must be new. Cover with hot water and bring to a boil. Simmer for 15 minutes, then cover and leave in hot water. Remove containers from the water about 5 minutes before using. They should be hot but dry.

Fill glasses or jars immediately; glasses to within ¼ inch of the top, jars to within ⅛ inch. If using paraffin, melt it in a small container with a lip until it is hot but not smoking. Pour a ⅛-inch layer over the top of jelly, tilting the glass so that the wax touches all outer edges. Lids should be placed on filled jars immediately and sealed according to manufacturer's instructions.

A thermometer is your best bet for timing the cooking of any preserve. Temperature is a vital factor in jelling, but since it is affected by weather and altitude, we recommend that you test the boiling point of water each day you preserve and adjust recipe temperatures accordingly (water boils at 212°F at sea level). Cook jellies to 8°F above the adjusted boiling point; jams and preserves need 9°F above boiling. Lacking a thermometer, you can test jelling by dipping ½ teaspoon of the hot liquid, cooling slightly, then slowly pouring back. If syrup does not form droplets, but falls in single sheet from the metal spoon, it's ready. Another test is to drop a spoonful onto a cold saucer; chill a few minutes to be sure it jells properly.

Jellies are made from fruit juice and sugar cooked together until the jelling point is reached. Pectin and acid both contribute to the jelling. Unripe fruit contains more pectin than overripe fruit, so select unblemished produce that is ripe but still firm and include some unripe fruit as well. Although apples, crab apples, currants, grapes, gooseberries, plums and cranberries are high in natural pectin, some cooks prefer to add commercial pectin, which comes in either liquid or powdered form, to assure a perfect jelly. Others combine low-pectin fruits, such as berries, with the juice of high-pectin fruits and add lemon juice to increase the acidity.

In addition to your large kettle and long-handled spoon, you will need a jelly bag made of cheesecloth or flannel (nap side in), a rack or colander to hold the bag and a large bowl to catch the juice. Do not squeeze the bag when straining juice for jelly or your finished product will be clouded. You will also need a ladle to fill the glasses.

To extract the juice from fruit, cover apples and other hard fruits with water and boil for 20 to 25 minutes; crush berries or grapes, add only enough cold water to prevent burning and cook about 10 minutes. Do not overcook or the flavor and pectin content will suffer. After the juice has been extracted, it is returned to the pot with sugar and cooked over moderate heat until the sugar dissolves. The heat is then raised and the mixture boiled rapidly until the jelling point (220°F at sea level) is reached.

Butters are made by cooking fruit pulp with sugar until the mixture is thick but spreadable. Pulp left after making jelly can be used or you can start from scratch. Preserves contain whole berries or large pieces of fruit and are not as thick as jams, which contain crushed or chopped fruits. Conserves are made from more than one fruit and generally have nuts or raisins added toward the end of cooking. Marmalades have pieces of fruit in a clear jelly. All should be cooked slowly until the sugar dissolves and then boiled rapidly until the jelling point for jams (221°F at sea level) is reached.

California Wine Jelly (page 191) and Mint Jelly (page 190)

MINT JELLY

Photograph on page 189

Makes about 3 pints

2 cups fresh mint leaves
2½ cups apple juice
2 tablespoons lemon juice
  Green food coloring
  (optional)

3½ cups C & H Granulated
  Sugar
1 packet liquid pectin

Wash mint leaves and place in large saucepan. Mash. Add apple juice. Bring to boil. Remove from heat, cover pan and let stand for 10 minutes. Strain. Add lemon juice and a few drops green food coloring. Measure 1¾ cups of this mixture. Combine with sugar in large pan. Bring back to full boil, stirring constantly. Stir in pectin, return to full boil for 1 minute, stirring constantly. Remove from heat. Skim off foam. Pour into hot sterilized jars. Seal immediately.

CRANBERRY JELLY

Makes about 2 pints

4 cups cranberries
2 cups water

2 cups C & H Granulated
  Sugar

Cook cranberries and water in saucepan until most of berries have burst. Force through coarse strainer. Return puree to saucepan, add sugar. Cook over low heat until sugar dissolves, swirling pan occasionally. Boil briskly, stirring frequently, to jelly stage (220°F on candy thermometer) or until syrup drops in a sheet from a metal spoon and is as thick as desired when tested on a cold saucer. Pour into hot sterilized jars. Seal immediately.

Note: For holiday and special occasions, mold in a ring and serve filled with Waldorf salad.

CALIFORNIA WINE JELLY

Photograph on page 189

Makes about 2 ½ pints

3 cups C & H Granulated Sugar

2 cups dry or sweet wine, sherry or port

1 packet liquid pectin

Combine sugar and wine in top of double boiler. Place over rapidly boiling water and heat 2 minutes or until sugar is dissolved, stirring constantly. Remove from heat and stir in liquid pectin at once. Pour into hot sterilized jars. Seal immediately.

Variation — Minted Wine Jelly: Use white port in recipe above. Add 10 to 12 drops mint extract plus green food coloring, if desired, to sugar and wine in double boiler. Or bring 1 ½ cups crushed mint leaves to boil in a pot with the wine and marinate until cool. Strain wine, remeasure, adding more wine if necessary, and follow recipe above.

Variation — Spiced Port Jelly: Use port in recipe above. Add ⅛ teaspoon EACH cinnamon *and* ground cloves to sugar and wine in double boiler. Follow recipe above.

QUINCE-APPLE-CRANBERRY JELLY

Makes about 4 pints

10 medium apples
5 quinces
4 cups (1 pound)
 cranberries

9 cups water
3 cups C & H Granulated
 Sugar

Wash fruit. Core and chop apples. Rub fuzz from quinces with cloth; core and chop. In 3 separate covered saucepans, cook quinces, apples and cranberries with 3 cups water each until soft. (Allow about 30 minutes for quinces, 20 minutes for apples and 10 minutes for cranberries.) Drain all fruits through several layers of dampened cheesecloth, squeezing and pressing with spoon. Combine juices. Measure 4 cups juice into large saucepan; add 3 cups sugar. Cook over low heat until sugar dissolves, swirling pan occasionally. Boil briskly, stirring frequently, to jelly stage (220°F on candy thermometer) or until syrup drops in a sheet from a metal spoon and is as thick as desired when tested on a cold saucer. Pour into hot sterilized jars. Seal immediately.

Repeat with equivalent amount of sugar for remaining juice.

PLUM JELLY

Makes about 2 pints

4 pounds fully ripe plums
 (preferably sour
 clingstone)

1 cup water
4 cups C & H Granulated
 Sugar

Crush plums with potato masher or food processor (do not peel or pit). Add water and bring to boil in large heavy kettle. Boil vigorously 10 minutes or until plums are tender, crushing occasionally. Ladle into jelly bag or large bowl lined with muslin towel that has been wrung out in cold water. Bring ends together, tie a loop around them and hang from hook until all juice drains out. Measure 4 cups juice into kettle. Add sugar. Stir constantly until mixture begins to boil. Boil vigorously without stirring until jelly stage (220°F on candy thermometer) or until syrup drops in a sheet from a metal spoon and is as thick as desired when tested on a cold saucer. Skim off any foam. Pour into hot sterilized jars. Seal immediately.

Note: Pectin Method — to 4 cups juice add 6½ cups C & H Granulated Sugar. Bring to a boil, stirring constantly. Immediately stir in 1 packet liquid pectin. Bring to full rolling boil for 1 minute, stirring constantly. Remove from heat. Skim off any foam. Bottle and seal.

Note: If sweet plums are used, substitute ¼ cup strained lemon juice for ½ cup plum juice.

CANTALOUPE PEACH MARMALADE

*Choose ginger or walnuts as the finishing touch for this
midsummer fruit medley*

Makes about 2½ pints

4 cups peeled, diced
     cantaloupe (2 to 2½
     pounds)
1 medium orange, minced
     (pulp and rind)
1 large lemon, minced
     (pulp and rind)
5 cups C & H Granulated
     Sugar

3 cups peeled, diced
     peaches (4 to 5
     medium)
½ teaspoon salt
3 tablespoons finely sliced
     crystallized ginger or
     ¾ cup coarsely
     chopped walnuts

In 6-quart kettle, combine cantaloupe, orange and lemon; slowly bring to a boil and cook for 10 minutes, stirring occasionally. Add sugar, peaches and salt. Boil briskly, stirring frequently, 20 minutes. Add ginger and cook 12 to 15 minutes longer, until syrup jells (220°F on candy thermometer) or is as thick as desired when tested on a cold saucer. Skim off any foam. Cool, stirring, 5 minutes. Ladle into hot sterilized jars to ⅛ inch from the top. Seal immediately.

THREE CITRUS MARMALADE

Makes 3 pints

2 large oranges
1 lime
1 lemon

6 cups water
5 cups C & H Granulated Sugar

Wash fruit. Cut in half lengthwise, then cut into very thin crosswise slices. Remove all seeds. Place fruit in large bowl. Add water and soak overnight. Place water and fruit in large saucepan. Bring to boil and cook until fruit is tender. Add sugar and stir until it dissolves. Boil briskly, stirring frequently, 15 to 30 minutes, until syrup jells (220°F on candy thermometer) or is as thick as desired when tested on a cold saucer. Skim off any foam. Ladle into hot sterilized jars to ⅛ inch from the top. Seal immediately.

APRICOT-PINEAPPLE-ALMOND MARMALADE

Makes about 3½ pints

6 cups fresh ripe apricots
6 cups C & H Granulated Sugar
1 cup canned crushed pineapple, drained

¼ teaspoon salt
1 large lemon or ½ orange
12 blanched almonds

Wash, halve and pit apricots. Combine sugar, apricots, pineapple and salt in large saucepan. Cut lemon in half lengthwise, trim off ends, then slice thin, discarding seeds. Add lemon slices to saucepan. Heat to boiling, stirring constantly, until sugar dissolves. Boil briskly, stirring frequently, about 20 minutes until syrup jells (220°F on candy thermometer) or is as thick as desired when tested on a cold saucer. Stir in almonds. Skim off any foam. Ladle into hot sterilized jars to ⅛ inch from the top. Seal immediately.

PEACH MARMALADE

*Make either the plain or spiced version to store up
peaches at their best*

Makes about 4 pints

3 pounds ripe peaches   C & H Granulated
   (12 medium)   Sugar
1 medium orange

Scald and peel peaches, remove pits; dice or mash. Place peaches
in large bowl. Squeeze juice from orange; discard pulp and grind
rind in food chopper or processor. Combine peaches, orange juice
and rind. Measure fruit mixture into heavy saucepan with an equal
amount of sugar. Heat to boiling, stirring constantly, until sugar dissolves. Boil briskly, stirring frequently, about 20 minutes, until syrup
jells (220°F on candy thermometer) or is as thick as desired when
tested on a cold saucer. Skim off any foam. Ladle into hot sterilized
jars to 1/8 inch from the top. Seal immediately.

Variation — Spicy Peach Marmalade: Substitute lemon for orange and add 1/4 teaspoon ground mace or nutmeg and 2 inches
stick cinnamon while cooking marmalade. Remove cinnamon before bottling.

RASPBERRY APRICOT JAM

Makes about 2 1/2 pints

1 1/2 cups raspberries   4 1/2 cups C & H Granulated
 20 fresh ripe apricots   Sugar
 1/4 cup water   Pinch of salt

Wash and drain raspberries. Wash, halve and pit apricots. Cook
apricots in water until soft. Add sugar, raspberries and salt. Stir until
sugar dissolves, then boil briskly, stirring frequently, about 30 minutes, until syrup jells (220°F on candy thermometer) or is as thick as
desired when tested on a cold saucer. Pour into shallow dish. Stir
occasionally while cooling. Leave overnight to plump fruit. Pack
cold in hot sterilized jars. Seal immediately.

THREE BERRY JAM

Makes about 2 pints

1 pint strawberries
1 pint blueberries or other
    berries
1 pint raspberries

C & H Granulated
    Sugar
Pinch of salt

Wash and drain berries, mash and measure into broad kettle or saucepan. Stir in 1 cup sugar for each cup mashed fruit. Add salt. Boil briskly 5 minutes, stirring almost constantly. Remove from heat and let stand in kettle about 12 hours, stirring occasionally, so that berries will plump up and not float. Pack cold in small, hot sterilized jars. Seal immediately.

HONEYDEW JAM

Savor that sweet melon taste on a cold winter day

Makes about 2 pints

2 limes
1 cup water
3 cups C & H Granulated
    Sugar

3 cups peeled, diced
    honeydew melon

Slice and seed limes; combine with water in blender or food processor. Process until limes are finely chopped. Pour into large saucepan, cover and cook 10 minutes. Add sugar and melon to limes. Heat to boiling, stirring constantly, until sugar dissolves. Boil briskly, stirring frequently, about 20 minutes or until syrup jells (220°F on candy thermometer) or is as thick as desired when tested on a cold saucer. Skim off any foam. Ladle into hot sterilized jars to ⅛ inch from the top. Seal immediately.

Three Berry Jam

APRICOT JAM

Makes about 2 pints (Do not double this recipe)

4 cups ripe apricots	2 tablespoons lemon juice
4 cups C & H Granulated Sugar	

Wash, halve and pit apricots; dice or mash. Combine half the sugar and all apricots in large saucepan. Cook over low heat until sugar dissolves, then boil hard 5 minutes, stirring constantly. Stir in lemon juice and remaining sugar. Boil briskly, stirring constantly, until syrup jells (220°F on candy thermometer) and is as thick as desired when tested on a cold saucer. Pour into shallow dish. Cool overnight, stirring occasionally, so that fruit will plump up and not float. Pack cold in hot sterilized jars. Seal immediately.

FRUIT BUTTERS

Whatever fruit you choose, store up its flavor with this easy preserve

Fruit — either:
  Apples — quartered; add equal amount of water
  Apricots or Peaches — skinned, pitted, crushed
  Plums — pitted, crushed
  Grapes — crushed
  Pears — stemmed, quartered; add half as much water as fruit
C & H Granulated Sugar
Cinnamon
Nutmeg
Salt

Prepare chosen fruit and cook in heavy saucepan until soft, stirring frequently. Force through strainer and measure puree. To each quart of fruit, add 1 cup sugar, ⅛ teaspoon cinnamon, ⅛ teaspoon nutmeg and pinch of salt. Return to pan and boil briskly, stirring frequently. As fruit butter thickens, reduce heat and cook until no liquid separates from pulp when mixture is placed on a cold saucer. Pour into hot sterilized jars to ⅛ inch from top. Seal immediately.

PEAR CONSERVE

Makes about 6 pints

3½ pounds pears
1½ large lemons
1½ large oranges
¼ cup raisins

7½ cups C & H Granulated Sugar
½ cup chopped walnuts

Peel and core pears. Chop citrus fruits; remove seeds but not rinds. Grind lemons, oranges, pears and raisins in food chopper or processor; drain off juice and discard. In large saucepan, cover fruit with sugar and marinate overnight. The next day, heat fruit mixture to boiling, stirring constantly, until sugar dissolves. Boil briskly about 35 minutes, until syrup jells (220°F on candy thermometer) or is as thick as desired when tested on a cold saucer. Stir in nuts. Skim off any foam. Ladle into hot sterilized jars to ⅛ inch from the top. Seal immediately.

PLUM CONSERVE

Lemon adds zip to this crunchy conserve

Makes about 2½ pints

3 cups C & H Granulated Sugar
4 cups chopped plums
Pinch of salt

Grated rind and juice of 1 lemon
¼ cup coarsely chopped walnuts or pecans

In large saucepan, combine sugar, plums, salt, lemon rind and juice. Heat to boiling, stirring constantly, until sugar dissolves. Boil briskly, stirring frequently, about 15 minutes until syrup jells (220°F on candy thermometer) or is as thick as desired when tested on a cold saucer. Stir in nuts. Skim off any foam. Ladle into hot sterilized jars to ⅛ inch from the top. Seal immediately.

Variation — Prune Conserve: Substitute prunes for plums in the recipe above.

199

GRAPE ORANGE CONSERVE

Makes about 5½ pints

4 pounds Concord or other slipskin grapes	**3** medium oranges
8 cups C & H Granulated Sugar	**2** lemons
	1 to **2** cups coarsely chopped walnuts

Wash grapes; squeeze pulp from skins (save skins). Cook pulp until seeds loosen, then press through wire strainer. Add skins and sugar to pulp. Squeeze juice from oranges and lemons; add to grapes. Carefully remove citrus rinds, taking as little of the white pith as possible; cut into fine strips. Cover rinds with cold water and heat to boiling. Drain and add to grapes. Simmer, stirring frequently, about 40 minutes, until thick. Add nuts. Ladle into hot sterilized jars. Seal immediately.

GINGER PEAR PRESERVES

Makes about 1½ pints

6 firm, ripe pears	**½** lemon, thinly sliced (pulp and rind)
2 cups C & H Granulated Sugar	**¼** cup preserved ginger, chopped

Peel, core and dice pears. Combine sugar, pears, and lemon in heavy saucepan. Heat to boiling, stirring constantly, until sugar dissolves. Boil briskly 10 minutes. Add ginger and continue boiling, stirring frequently, until syrup jells (220°F on candy thermometer). Mixture should be thick but still "runny." Skim off any foam. Ladle into hot sterilized jars to ⅛ inch from the top. Seal immediately.

Grape Orange Conserve

PEACH PLUM PRESERVES

This tangy combination will perk up your toast

Makes about 3 pints

3 cups sliced tart plums
(about 1½ pounds)

3 cups sliced, peeled
peaches or pears
(about 1½ pounds)

½ lemon, minced (pulp
and rind)

5 cups C & H Granulated
Sugar

Combine fruits and half of sugar in 6-quart kettle. Cook over low heat, stirring to draw juice. Add remaining sugar. Boil briskly, stirring constantly about 15 minutes, until syrup jells (220°F on candy thermometer) or is as thick as desired when tested on a cold saucer. Skim off any foam. Cool, stirring, 5 minutes. Ladle into hot sterilized jars to ⅛ inch from the top. Seal immediately.

BRANDIED PEACH PRESERVES

Makes about 4 pints

5 cups C & H Granulated
Sugar

1 cup cold water

10 large firm-ripe peaches

6 whole cloves

½ cup good quality brandy

¾ cup chopped walnuts or
pecans

In large heavy saucepan, combine 1½ cups of the sugar and the water. Cook over low heat until sugar dissolves, swirling pan occasionally. Scald, peel, pit and quarter peaches. Add to sugar and simmer gently about 25 minutes, until transparent. With slotted spoon, remove peaches from syrup. Add remaining sugar and the cloves. Cook over low heat until sugar dissolves, then boil until reduced to a thick syrup. Stir in brandy. Sieve syrup over peaches; add nuts. Ladle peaches into hot sterilized jars. Cover with hot syrup to ⅛ inch from the top. Seal immediately.

CHERRY PRESERVES

Makes about 1 ½ pints

**2 cups C & H Granulated
Sugar
½ cup water**

**Pinch of salt
2 cups pitted sour cherries**

In large saucepan, combine 1 cup sugar, the water and salt. Cook over low heat until sugar dissolves, swirling pan occasionally. Boil until syrup reaches 236°F on candy thermometer (soft ball stage). Add 1 cup cherries; boil 10 minutes. Add remaining sugar and cherries and boil 10 minutes longer. Cool in pan, stirring occasionally to plump cherries. Ladle into hot sterilized jars to ⅛ inch from the top. Seal immediately.

RHU-BERRY PRESERVES

Makes about 2 pints

**4 cups C & H Granulated
Sugar
3 cups sliced rhubarb
2 cups raspberries or
strawberries**

**Grated rind *and* juice of
1 orange *and* ½ lemon**

Combine all ingredients in large kettle. Heat to boiling, stirring constantly, until sugar dissolves. Boil briskly, stirring frequently, about 10 minutes until syrup jells (220°F on candy thermometer) or is as thick as desired when tested on a cold saucer. Skim off any foam. Ladle into hot sterilized jars to ⅛ inch from the top. Seal immediately. Store in cool, dry, dark place.

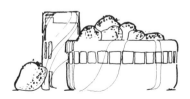

APPLE PRESERVES

Makes about 4 pints

6 cups C & H Granulated
  Sugar
  Pinch of salt
1 tablespoon EACH
  grated orange *and*
  lemon rind

¼ cup lemon juice
1¾ cups water
9 medium apples

In large saucepan, combine sugar, salt, orange rind, lemon rind, lemon juice and water. Cook over low heat until sugar dissolves, swirling pan occasionally. Boil gently 5 minutes. Wash, quarter and core, but do not pare apples. Dice or grate and add to hot syrup. Simmer gently, stirring occasionally, for 1 hour or until apples are transparent and syrup is rich and thick. Skim off any foam. Ladle into hot sterilized jars to ⅛ inch from the top. Seal immediately.

OLD-TIMER TOMATO PRESERVES

Makes 2½ pints

3 pounds firm, ripe red or
  yellow tomatoes
4½ cups C & H Granulated
  Sugar

¼ teaspoon salt
2 lemons, thinly sliced
3 inches stick cinnamon

Scald, peel and quarter tomatoes. With hands, gently squeeze out and discard seeds and excess juice. Add sugar and salt to tomato pulp and marinate overnight. Next day, drain juice into large saucepan; add lemons and cinnamon. Boil rapidly until syrup spins a thread (232°F on candy thermometer). Add tomatoes and simmer gently until transparent. Cool in pan, stirring occasionally. Ladle into hot sterilized jars to ⅛ inch from the top. Seal immediately.

9 DECORATE THAT CAKE

It's fun, creative—and says you care

Even the simplest cake can be a creative monument when it's lovingly decorated for a special occasion. We've used two techniques for decorating the cake on page 207—sugar molding and a pastry bag with tips.

SUGAR MOLDING

To Mold Sugar: Measure 5 cups C & H Granulated Sugar into glass or ceramic bowl. Add 1 egg white or 2 tablespoons water. Rub mixture between palms until thoroughly blended and cohesive. Add more water if necessary. For various colors, divide into separate bowls, add a few drops food coloring to each bowl; rub again until color is evenly mixed. Keep bowls covered with damp towels.

Pack sugar very firmly into each dry mold. Level off surface with straight knife. Place piece of cardboard over mold and invert; lift off mold, tapping to loosen if necessary. If shape falls apart, sugar is too dry and needs a few drops more water. If shape sticks to mold, mixture is too wet and needs a little more sugar. Molds that are to be used repeatedly should be dusted with cornstarch.

Let shapes dry at room temperature for 45 minutes to one hour, until crust hardens. To hasten drying, place in sunlight or put in preheated 200°F oven 5 minutes. The shapes can be hollowed out with a teaspoon and the scooped-out sugar reused. The dampened sugar mixture can be kept for a few days in a tightly covered container for reuse.

CAKE FROSTINGS AND ICINGS

Consult the index and select a frosting that appeals to you. Any of the buttercreams are good for frosting your cake. So is the Cocoa Fluff Frosting. Plan your design. Use colors suitable to the type of cake you are decorating. Divide and color icing to fit the pattern. Following are two icings, each excellent for decorating.

Basic Decorating Icing

Makes about 2½ cups

4 cups C & H Powdered
    Sugar
½ cup shortening

¼ cup water
1 teaspoon flavoring
    (optional)

Combine all ingredients in bowl. Mix at medium speed 8 to 10 minutes. Keep icing covered when not using. Store in refrigerator.

Decorating Icing No. 2

Makes 4 cups

4 cups C & H Powdered
    Sugar
1 cup shortening

1 egg white
½ teaspoon flavoring
    (optional)

Combine all ingredients in mixing bowl. Beat at medium speed at least 10 minutes. Scrape beaters and side of bowl several times to mix well. Keep in covered container.

PASTRY BAGS AND TUBES

To Make Decorating Bags: You need at least one bag for each color icing you use, and if more than one tip is used for a particular color, you'll need a bag for each tip. For our birthday cake, we used five bags.

1. Cut 12-inch square of waxed paper. Fold into triangle.

2. Holding thumb at A, fold a cone making sure points at top overlap.

3. Fasten at top by folding over several times or taping.

4. Cut off 1 inch at point. Drop tube into bag so that it protrudes at opening at bottom of bag.

5. Fill with frosting, not over ⅔ full.

6. Close top by folding over 2 or 3 times and tucking in ends.

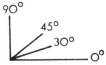

Squeeze frosting down to fill tube. Continue folding top down as tube empties.

To Make Star Border: Use tip No. 21 and hold the bag at 90° angle to cake. Pipe out individual stars.

To Make Zigzag Border: Use tip No. 21 and hold bag at 30° angle to cake. Pipe out a continuous border.

To Make Leaves: Use tip No. 67 and hold bag at 45° angle to cake.

To Write: Use tip No. 3 and hold bag at 45° angle to cake. The icing may need to be thinned down a little with a few drops of milk or water. If icing sticks in tube, use a pin to unclog it.

To Make Roses: Fasten a 1½-inch square of waxed paper on center of decorating nail with a small dot of icing. Hold nail between thumb and forefinger in left hand, decorating bag in right hand. Rotate nail counter-clockwise as you apply pressure on decorating bag. Nail should rotate as petals are being formed. It takes practice; be patient.

1. Using tip No. 104, make a dome of icing, holding tube straight down.

2. With narrow opening of tube up for this and remaining steps, circle icing around dome, tilting tube at 45° angle.

3. Circle icing up, around and down to make a high cone, tilting tube at 45° angle.

4. Start half way up cone, pipe 3 petals around cone, holding tube at 90° angle.

5. Pipe 4 petals under first row, tilting tube at 45° angle.

6. Finish with 5 to 7 petals around base of cone, holding tube at 30° angle.

Use waxed paper to remove rose to plate. Refrigerate for about 20 minutes before removing from paper with knife to place on cake.

C & H ANNIVERSARY CAKE

The grand cake pictured on our cover and on page 212 has been especially created by Bo Friberg, pastry chef of the California Culinary Academy in honor of C and H Sugar Company's 75th Anniversary. In designing this celebration cake, Chef Friberg chose a recipe that would be elegant to behold and, at the same time, within reach of the novice to prepare. Although the cake requires careful assembly and is composed of more parts than any of our other desserts, it can be done with patience. Each of the components can be prepared one or two days in advance and the entire cake can be put together early on the day of the party when there are no distractions. For spectacular results that will gratify the cook as well as the guests, read the directions several times before beginning and proceed one step at a time.

Makes 25 to 30 servings

Sponge Cake (page 213)	Chocolate Buttercream (page 215)
Pastry Cream (page 213)	18 ounces semisweet dark chocolate
Marzipan (page 214) including sign, leaves and flowers	1 egg white Food coloring

For easier handling, prepare Marzipan several days beforehand and Sponge Cake and Pastry Cream the day before cake is to be assembled. Chocolate Buttercream can also be prepared the day before, if desired. Top and bottom layers of cake are both obtained from a single 17-inch layer. To create smaller top layer, place a 10-inch cardboard circle in center of cake. Cut around it with a knife. With 2 spatulas, lift out a 10-inch cake, leaving a 17-inch "doughnut" cake base with a hole in the middle.

Cut off any crust from the tops and sides of the 10- and 17-inch cakes, then slice each cake into 3 even horizontal layers. Place the bottom layer of the 10-inch cake on the 10-inch cardboard. Cut out a 17-inch piece of cardboard and place the bottom layer of the larger cake on it; put both on a serving plate which has been lined with waxed paper. (The waxed paper will be slipped out after the cake is decorated, leaving a clean plate.)

Spread ¼-inch thickness of Pastry Cream on bottom 17-inch sponge layer. Put on second layer and spread with ¼-inch thickness of Chocolate Buttercream. Put on top layer and frost sides and top of layers with buttercream. Repeat procedure for 10-inch layers, reserving ½ cup buttercream to attach decorations later.

To support the 10-inch cake on the 17-inch layers, cut out several pieces of cardboard and glue together into a triangular brace that comes even with top of hole in 17-inch layers. Fill "doughnut" hole with brace.

On counter sprinkled with powdered sugar, roll out ¹⁄₁₆-inch-thick circles of Marzipan large enough to fit on top of each cake. Trim off excess.

Melt remaining 16 ounces of chocolate and cool to 105°F (luke-warm). Spread thin layer of melted chocolate over top and sides of cake. To insure a satin shine, work and spread icing until it shows signs of hardening. If chocolate sits on cake too long before it hardens, it will turn grey. Carefully place smaller cake on large base. Refrigerate several hours to set up.

To hide place where 17- and 10-inch layers are joined, roll out Marzipan and cut out one 11- and one 18-inch strip, each ½ inch wide. Decorate the strips by etching evenly spaced indentations with back of a knife. Paint back of strips with egg white so they will stick to cake. Wrap 11-inch strip where cakes are joined and 18-inch strip around bottom of cake. Line up Marzipan edges and cut off excess. Decorate cake with Marzipan Sign, Leaves and Flowers, attaching them with dabs of leftover Chocolate Buttercream or Chocolate Icing that are spooned on or piped through pastry bag.

Sponge Cake

1 cup (2 sticks) butter	17 eggs, room temperature
2¼ cups C & H Granulated Sugar	2¾ cups high-gluten or bread flour, sifted

Preheat oven to 375°F. Butter and flour 17-inch cake pan.* Melt butter and set aside to cool. Beat sugar and eggs together at high speed 5 minutes, until thick. Reduce to medium speed and beat 10 minutes longer, until mixture triples in volume and turns a pale lemon color. Fold in flour and butter alternately, working carefully so mixture doesn't lose volume. Pour into cake pan. Bake 20 to 25 minutes until cake tester inserted into center comes out clean or cake springs back when center is gently pushed in with index finger. Cool on rack. Chill overnight to firm cake for filling and frosting.

*Note: 17-inch cake pans can be purchased where cake decorating supplies are sold or ordered from Maid of Scandinavia (3245 Raleigh Avenue, Minneapolis, MN 55416). This sponge cake could also be baked in two 10-inch layer pans.

Variation—Chocolate Sponge Cake: Substitute ¾ cup cocoa for 1 cup of the bread flour. Sift flour and cocoa together before folding into egg mixture.

Pastry Cream

1 cup plus 2 tablespoons C & H Granulated Sugar	Pinch of salt
	1 quart milk
½ cup cornstarch, sifted	1 teaspoon vanilla
3 eggs, room temperature	C & H Granulated Sugar

Combine 1 cup plus 2 tablespoons sugar, the cornstarch, eggs and salt. Beat until thick and lemon colored. Meanwhile, bring milk to boil in large heavy saucepan. Slowly pour milk into sugar mixture, beating constantly. Return to saucepan. With a wooden spatula, stir constantly over low heat until mixture is as thick as pudding. Do not let boil. Stir in vanilla and sprinkle with sugar so crust doesn't form. When cool, refrigerate.

213

Marzipan

2½ cups C & H Powdered Sugar
1¾ cups almond paste

2½ tablespoons light corn syrup or glucose

Blend sugar, almond paste and corn syrup in stainless steel or ceramic bowl (copper or aluminum will discolor mixture) until ingredients hold together. Refrigerate until ready to use (wrapped airtight, it will last for months in the refrigerator). When ready, bring Marzipan to room temperature; knead in droplets of water to soften as necessary.

Marzipan Sign: Measure ¼ cup (packed) Marzipan. Roll out ⅛-inch thick and cut out 2 ovals. Melt 2 ounces of the semisweet dark chocolate. Spread a small amount of chocolate on back of 1 oval, sandwich with second oval and dry overnight. The next day, remelt leftover chocolate to decorate sign. Add water, no more than 3 drops at a time or chocolate will lump (you may need 20 to 25 drops), until chocolate is of spreading consistency. Put in paper decorating cone and pipe out border and message on front of oval.

Marzipan Leaves: Measure ½ cup (packed) Marzipan and add desired amount of green coloring. Knead until smooth. Roll out ¹⁄₁₆-inch thick. Cut out leaves with sharp paring knife dipped in oil. With back of knife, draw leaf veins. Gently bend leaves over a rolling pin to curve and dry.

Marzipan Flowers: Measure 1 cup (packed) Marzipan, add desired coloring and knead until smooth. Roll into a log about ½-inch in diameter and slice pieces ¼- to ½-inch wide for desired number of flowers. Allow 4 pieces for regular flowers, 6 to 8 pieces for large flowers. Roll each piece into a ball; flatten slightly with your hand and place 2 inches apart at the edge of the table. Using an oiled light bulb, thin the top of each piece. Cut thin side into "petals." Using 1 piece as a center bud, overlap remaining pieces around it.

Chocolate Buttercream

2¼ cups C & H Granulated Sugar
1 cup (8) egg whites, room temperature

2½ cups (5 sticks) butter, softened
4 ounces semisweet dark chocolate

Combine sugar and egg whites in mixing bowl. Place mixing bowl in another bowl of simmering water and beat until sugar dissolves and mixture feels warm to finger. Remove from water bath and beat at high speed until stiff peaks form. Working very quickly to prevent lumps, beat butter into egg mixture a little at a time. Beat 5 minutes longer, occasionally scraping down sides of bowl. While beating, melt chocolate in top of double boiler. When chocolate is at least 105°F (lukewarm), stir into buttercream.

METRIC IN THE KITCHEN

When you shop for new kitchen implements, look for products that give you metric equivalents. Once the confusion of converting is over, we think you'll enjoy working with the more precise metric system. A liter is always a liter, whether iiquid or dry. In our current system, a cup of milk is 8 ounces but a cup of sugar may weigh less than 4 ounces!

During the transition period, many kitchen metrics will be rounded off as follows:

APPROXIMATE EQUIVALENTS

1 inch	= 2.5 centimeters (cm)
1 ounce	= 30 grams (g)
1 pound	= 500 g = 0.5 kilogram (kg)
1 teaspoon	= 5 milliliters (ml)
1 tablespoon	= 15 ml
1 cup	= 250 ml
1 pint	= 500 ml
1 quart	= 1 liter (L)

TEMPERATURE: Fahrenheit vs. Celsius

(freezing)	32°F	= 0°C
(boiling)	212°F	= 100°C
	300°F	= 149°C
	350°F	= 175°C
	400°F	= 205°C
	450°F	= 230°C

EQUIVALENTS

apples, 1 pound	= 3 cups peeled and sliced
apricots, dried, 1 pound	= 3 cups
bananas, 3 to 4 medium	= 1¾ cups mashed
butter, 1 pound	= 2 cups
whipped, 1 pound	= 3 cups
1 stick	= ½ cup or 8 tablespoons
chocolate, unsweetened, 1 square	= 1 ounce
chips, 6 ounces	= 1 cup
cranberries, 1 pound	= 4 cups sauce
cream, whipping, 1 cup	= 2 cups whipped
dates, 1 pound	= 2½ cups pitted and chopped
eggs, 6 medium	= 1 cup
gelatin, 1 package plain	= 1 tablespoon
graham crackers, 12	= 1 cup crushed
lemon, 1 medium	= 2 tablespoons juice and 1¼ teaspoons grated rind
lime, 1 medium	= 1½ teaspoons juice and ¾ teaspoon grated rind
molasses, 12 ounces	= 1½ cups
nuts, ¼ pound meats	= 1 cup chopped
orange, 1 medium	= 7 tablespoons juice and 1½ tablespoons grated rind
peaches, 4 medium	= 2 cups peeled and sliced
pears, 4 medium	= 2 cups peeled and sliced
pecans in shell, 1 pound	= 2¼ cups shelled
prunes, dried, 1 pound	= 2½ cups pitted, or 2 cups cooked, drained
pumpkin, canned, 16 ounces	= 2 cups
raisins, seedless, 1 pound	= 2¾ cups
seeded, 1 pound	= 3¼ cups
shortening, hydrogenated, 1 pound	= 2⅓ cups
strawberries, 1 quart	= 4 cups hulled and sliced
walnuts in shell, 1 pound	= 2 cups shelled
yeast, 1 cake compressed	= ⅗ ounce
active dry, 1 package	= 1 tablespoon

SUBSTITUTIONS

In times of emergency, here are some substitutions that can be made when a recipe calls for an ingredient that's not on your shelf.

For	**Use**
1 teaspoon baking powder	$1/2$ teaspoon cream of tartar + $1/4$ teaspoon baking soda
$1/2$ cup (1 stick) butter or margarine	7 tablespoons vegetable shortening
1 ounce unsweetened chocolate	3 tablespoons cocoa + 1 tablespoon butter or margarine
1 cup grated coconut	$1 1/3$ cups flaked coconut
1 cup light cream	$7/8$ cup whole milk + 3 tablespoons butter
1 cup sour cream	1 tablespoon lemon juice + evaporated milk to make 1 cup (let stand 5 minutes)
1 cup whipping cream (for cooking)	$3/4$ cup whole milk + $1/3$ cup butter
2 egg yolks	1 whole egg
2 tablespoons flour	1 tablespoon cornstarch, arrowroot, potato starch or quick-cooking tapioca
1 cup honey or corn syrup	$1 1/4$ cups C & H Granulated Sugar + $1/4$ cup water
1 teaspoon lemon juice	$1/2$ teaspoon white vinegar
1 teaspoon grated lemon rind	$1/2$ teaspoon lemon extract
1 cup milk	1 cup skim milk + 2 tablespoons butter or margarine
	$1/2$ cup evaporated milk + $1/2$ cup water
	$1/4$ cup powdered whole milk + 1 cup water
1 cup buttermilk or sour milk	1 tablespoon lemon juice or white vinegar + whole milk to make 1 cup (let stand 5 minutes)
1 cup yogurt	1 cup buttermilk

INDEX

Recipes printed in blue indicate they are quick and easy to prepare.